With a Little Help
from My Friends

With a Little Help from My Friends

Conversation-Based Instruction for Culturally and Linguistically Diverse (CLD) Classrooms

Paula J. Mellom
Rebecca K. Hixon
Jodi P. Weber

TEACHERS COLLEGE PRESS

TEACHERS COLLEGE | COLUMBIA UNIVERSITY

NEW YORK AND LONDON

Published by Teachers College Press, 1234 Amsterdam Avenue, New York, NY 10027

Copyright © 2019 by Teachers College, Columbia University

Cover design by Ellen Walker / ELWalkerDesign.

Library of Congress Cataloging-in-Publication Data is available at loc.gov

ISBN 978-0-8077-6156-4 (paper)
ISBN 978-0-8077-6178-6 (hardcover)
ISBN 978-0-8077-7797-8 (ebook)

Printed on acid-free paper
Manufactured in the United States of America

Contents

Acknowledgments

We are honored to have worked with so many talented and innovative teachers across the state of Georgia, whose contributions to the enhancement of the pedagogy and development of the tools for implementation are too vast to enumerate. This remarkable group of teachers has demonstrated a passion and commitment that has surpassed expectations, and we are grateful. We would be remiss if we didn't give a particular nod of appreciation to Niki Hill. Though many teachers did extraordinary work both off and on camera, the video of students in Niki's classroom engaged in an Instructional Conversation (IC) (see coe.uga.edu/directory/latino-achievement) has become one of our most powerful tools to help educators get a quick sense of what collaborative, conversation-based instruction looks like. Thank you, Niki!

We are humbled by the trust that key superintendents and administrators have invested in us from the start, and that has continued to strengthen over the years. During the Center for Latino Achievement and Success in Education's (CLASE) federally funded IES randomized controlled trial, district superintendents recognized the value of relevant research in their classrooms and the rigor that CLASE and the University of Georgia would bring to such an initiative. Principals welcomed us into their schools and classrooms and provided us with critical information that has allowed us to contextualize our work and pursue system-specific research questions. Among the many dedicated and passionate teams of educators who have worked with us on this project, three school districts have been with us from the start and have continued to sustain the CLASE Instructional Conversation work, engaging us to a higher level after the federal grant ended in order to train more of their teachers. In doing so, they have provided us with the highest level of praise education researchers can aspire to.

These districts, in alphabetical order, are:

Barrow County School System
Superintendent: Dr. Chris McMichael
English Learner Support Coordinator: Julie Eldridge

Gwinnett County Public Schools
CEO/Superintendent: J. Alvin Wilbanks
English Language Learner Programs Director: Dr. Elizabeth Webb

Habersham County Schools
Superintendent: Matthew Cooper
Director of Elementary Schools: Rhonda Andrews

In large part due to their confidence in us, our work has continued to flourish, allowing us to reach out to more school districts in our state, as well as nationally and internationally. We are truly honored by their willingness to continually collaborate with us in an iterative, reciprocal relationship that benefits from, and depends on, the input of all stakeholders. We work hard to maintain their confidence in us.

We are grateful to the large number of graduate students and instructional coaches who have diligently collected and analyzed data, observed teachers and provided feedback, alerted us to the great work of individual teachers, and helped to develop many of the tools that we have adapted for observation, professional development, and research. Without these hard-working, dedicated professionals, the pedagogy and the tools used to implement it would not be as robust as they are today.

We would like to give special recognition to Dr. Diego Boada, who has been the fourth member of our team, diligently working to make this model accessible through various digital resources, and the developer of our Instructional Conversation Online Platform—an online Community of Practice for the over 800 teachers who have attended one of our IC Foundational Institute Trainings thus far. This piece has been vital in the growing of this model and offers a space for IC trained teachers to collaborate with one another across districts (and even countries!), sharing resources and ideas to further the sustainable implementation of ICs in today's classrooms.

Finally, we would like to thank the Executive Director of CLASE, Dr. Pedro Portes. Without his vision of applying the gold standard of a multisite randomized controlled trial (RCT) to examine the effectiveness of Instructional Conversations in classrooms, our outreach into schools and the professional development that has ensued would never have occurred. Thank you, Dr. Portes, for your support and faith in us as well as your continued leadership in researching the fidelity of implementation and validity of the tools we have developed.

Two final notes: If we have neglected to mention individuals who have made valuable contributions to our work, we apologize. Our oversight is not intentional, nor does it reflect any lack of gratitude. And although we owe much of our thinking and growth in theory and practice to the extended team of educators and researchers who have partnered with us, any errors or flaws in the work are entirely ours.

Paula J. Mellom
Rebecca K. Hixon
Jodi P. Weber

Preface

SOCIOCULTURAL CONTEXT OF TODAY AND
WHY WE NEED THIS CONVERSATION-BASED SYSTEM

While the number of students enrolled in schools in the United States has remained relatively static, the number and percentage of English learners (ELs) and students who speak languages other than English enrolled in U.S. schools has increased dramatically in recent years (NCELA, 2017; NCES, 2015; Passel, Cohn, & Lopez, 2011; U.S. Census Bureau, 2010) with ELs currently accounting for approximately 10% of all enrolled students nationwide (NCELA, 2018). The South and the Midwest have been particularly impacted by this growth; in the so-called "new immigrant" states, such as Georgia, where we have done most of our work, the growth has been exponential, with an overall increase in ELs of 247% and up to 600% in some counties in just 10 years (Hooker, Fix, & McHugh, 2014). Across the nation, this growth in ELs has put an unprecedented strain on the national teacher corps, over 80% of which is white, monolingual, and female (U.S. Census Bureau, 2010). The resulting cultural and linguistic disconnect between the student population and their teachers is exacerbated by the fact that few of these teachers have the experience or training in culturally responsive pedagogies that could help them address the unique challenges faced by culturally and linguistically diverse (CLD) students. This situation has real and potentially devastating implications for all students' educational success.

This disconnect between teacher preparation and student needs happens at a time when mediated communication (the use of emails, texting, and social media, etc.) has begun to eclipse face-to-face communication, and there is a growing concern that the skill of engaging in conversation and civil discourse has become a lost art form. Students graduate and enter the workforce lacking the skills to collaborate, communicate, and problem-solve effectively, while businesses are demanding these skills of successful job applicants. These "soft skills" are becoming more and more critical to individual, social, and business success because they are necessary to address the increasingly complex challenges that society faces and will face in the future, especially as so many of these challenges, and the jobs designed to address them, do not yet exist. As educators focus their attention on college and career readiness, the result is a clarion call for us to change the way we teach in order to better prepare our students.

The purpose of this text is to introduce teachers to a research-based system for collaborative, conversation-based instruction that positively impacts all students' (but particularly English learners') ability to communicate, collaborate, and problem-solve, while offering spaces for teachers to formatively assess and differentiate instruction to meet the varying needs of their students.

To develop our system for collaborative, conversation-based instruction, we draw primarily on research grounded in sociocultural and constructivist theory, as developed in the fields of education, linguistics, second language acquisition, cognitive science, and psychology. Psychologist Lev Vygotsky (1978) posited that variables such as interaction, culture, and language impact cognitive development and learning. In the field of second language acquisition, researchers have found that innate ability and exposure to language alone cannot explain language acquisition, but that interaction with other speakers is essential to language learning (Lantolf, Thorne, & Poehner, 2015; Long, 1983; Van Lier, 2014). Children learn the "rules" of language through interaction with adults and peers (Bruner & Haste, 2010), and students learn better if they have to "negotiate" for meaning (Long, 1983). Further, students learn more when they are "pushed" to produce a product or "output" (Swain & Lapkin, 1995). Constructivist theories suggest that opportunities to reflect on previously constructed schemata and wrangle with conceptual conflicts in real and applied ways is how knowledge is constructed and reconstructed (Derry, 1996). The Instructional Conversation pedagogical model laid out in this text is grounded in these theoretical foundations; however, we also borrow from research looking at the topics of collaboration and conversation in such disparate fields as sociology, social work, medicine, and even business. We will discuss these more throughout the text.

EVOLUTION OF THE ARCH MODEL FOR COLLABORATIVE CONVERSATION-BASED INSTRUCTION

There are many student-centered pedagogies and curricular design methodologies that focus on collaborative learning and the development of critical thinking skills (e.g., problem-based learning) and many other conversation-based pedagogies (e.g., Harkness Model, Socratic Seminars, etc.); however, few attempt to systematically integrate collaboration and conversation together, and even fewer anchor that integration around a problem or product. The Arch system for collaborative, conversation-based instruction that we outline in this text is rooted in the Five Standards for Effective Pedagogy developed by the Center for Research for Education, Diversity, and Excellence (CREDE) at the University of California–Berkeley. In the chapters that follow, we will describe in depth the system and tools that we have developed; but before we begin, it is important to understand the theoretical underpinnings on which this system is grounded, and the journey we have taken to connect these abstract theoretical ideas to practice and help them come alive in real and applied ways in today's diverse classrooms.

After an exhaustive meta-study of more than 30 years of research into pedagogical practice, CREDE found that there were five critical standards that most impacted diverse learners (Tharp, Estrada, Dalton, & Yamauchi, 2000). Grounded in sociocultural perspectives of teaching and learning, these pedagogical standards represent guiding principles for teaching that are good for all students, but especially helpful for those students placed at risk due to linguistic or cultural factors. Standard I is *Teacher and Student Producing Together*, described as "facilitat[ing] learning through joint productive activity (JPA) among teacher and students using multiple activity settings and student groupings" (Dalton, 2008, p. 51). Indicators for this standard include creating a classroom community agreement, arranging the classroom and grouping the students to promote interaction, and designing a JPA. Standard II is *Developing Language and Literacy,* described as "develop[ing] competence in the language and literacy of instruction across the curriculum" (Dalton, 2008, p. 97). Indicators for this standard include affirming student language preferences, expanding expression, and providing phonics and comprehension activities that lead to literacy. Standard III is *Connecting School to Students' Lives* and is described as "connect[ing] teaching and curriculum to students' experiences at home and in the community" (Dalton, 2008, p. 133). Indicators for this standard include linking learning to students' lives, contextualizing academic topics, and differentiating the activities to meet the needs of the students. Standard IV is *Teaching Complex Thinking* and is described as "challeng[ing] students to think at increasingly complex levels" (Dalton, 2008, p. 159). Classroom indicators for this standard include setting high standards, assisting students as they perform at higher levels, and teaching challenging content. The final standard, Standard V, is *Teaching through Conversation*, and is described as "engag[ing] students in dialogue, especially instructional conversation (IC)"

(Dalton, 2008, p. 189). Indicators for this standard include making ICs part of the classroom routine and guiding the students to full participation.

In 2010, the Center for Latino Achievement and Success in Education (CLASE) was awarded a $2.9 million dollar grant by the U.S. Department of Education to conduct a randomized controlled trial to test the efficacy of Instructional Conversations in 3rd- and 5th-grade classrooms across the state of Georgia—in rural, urban, and suburban districts. During the grant, the focus of the research was the implementation of the fifth standard—Instructional Conversations (ICs)—and how these small group teacher-facilitated interactions impacted student achievement. Although the other four standards were highly encouraged during these ICs, the emphasis was specifically on the application of these standards during small-group inter-actions, not classroom-wide. Results showed that Instructional Conversa-tions do, in fact, positively impact the academic achievement of ELs and all learners (Portes, González-Canché, Boada, & Whatley, 2018). These results indicate that while Instructional Conversations are good for all kids, they may make a critical difference for ELs.

Given the demands on classrooms today, our work in providing profes-sional development has widened beyond the scope of the research to focus on *how* to create tools and structures that enable the facilitation of ICs, and all five of the standards, in a systematic way. These systematic structures not only clarify and encourage the application of these standards during ICs, but through all modes of instruction (i.e., whole group, small group, paired work), and create a critical path to teacher and student success.

One of the points of clarification involved a reorganization in the way we present the standards. In response to some confusion caused by the language in CREDE's definitions (see Gokee, 2017), CLASE's mod-el has attempted to clarify the presentation of the work, and thereby reduce the confusion of "Instructional Conversation" as both a process—teaching through conversation—and a thing—a small-group, teacher-facilitated event. Most notably, we have separated out "Purposeful Conver-sation" as its own Standard (representing the *process* of teaching through conversation), and identified an Instructional Conversation (IC) as a specific type of Joint Productive Activity (JPA), in which the students are engaged in a teacher-facilitated instructional activity where collaboration and con-versation are required to complete a product. (See Figure P.1 for a graphic representation of this reorganization of the Five Standards.)

Through our work, we found that what holds the Five Standards to-gether as a system is the Joint Productive Activity (JPA), with the Instruc-tional Conversation (IC) being a very specific kind of JPA where the teacher is present to facilitate and enhance the impact of each of the Five Standards,

Figure P.1. The Five Standards Reorganized

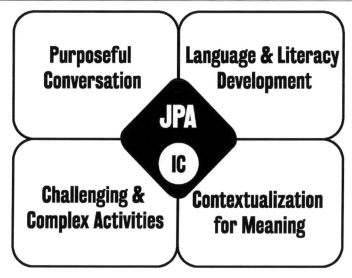

as well as to differentiate and elevate the level of instruction. While each of the standards is vital and supports the systematic structure, Purposeful Conversation is perhaps the most critical after the Joint Productive Activity (JPA) because it is through purposeful conversation that the teacher can incorporate all of the standards and increase the complexity of activities, elevate and assess language and literacy development, and contextualize lessons for meaning.

From this introduction to the standards, readers may be thinking, "This is just good teaching. I already do most of this!" While most of the individual concepts shouldn't sound completely foreign, we have found that these concepts can be deceptively difficult to implement effectively as a *system*. Through our ongoing collaboration with teachers, instructional coaches, and administrators, we have developed a structure with tools for implementation, observation, and coaching to facilitate sustained and integrated application of these five standards. As we move forward in this text, we will discuss theory and research that support these standards and how teachers have applied and implemented their use in classrooms. We have worked with over 800 teachers across 29 systems in two countries. We guided them in the theoretical underpinnings, the strength of the research, and assured fidelity of implementation through observations and feedback, and they in turn have guided us in the specifics of how to make it work in real classrooms with real students. Regardless of the age, gender, cultural or socioeconomic background, diagnosis, label, or previous school experience of

---

FOOD FOR THOUGHT

Consider the following quote and how this might apply to your students.

> To instruct someone . . . is not a matter of getting him to commit results to mind. Rather, it is to teach him to participate in the process that makes possible the establishment of knowledge. We teach a subject not to produce little living libraries on that subject, but rather to get a student to think mathematically for himself, to consider matters as an historian does, to take part in the process of knowledge-getting. Knowing is a process not a product. (*The Process of Education: Towards a Theory of Instruction,* Bruner, 1966, p. 72)

Questions to Consider

- What does it mean to say that "knowing is a process not a product"?
- How often do we teachers ask students a question and when they reply with the "expected" answer, respond "Very good!" and move on? What is the impact of this?
- How can we slow down or change our questions to allow students to explain their thinking and thereby open a window into the process of learning for us and other students?

---

the student; regardless of the size, urban, suburban, or agrarian location of the school; regardless of the years of experience, path of entry into the field, certifications, endorsements, or content area focus of the teachers, we saw growth.

We will also be discussing these five standards as a system and how they work together to construct a model for classroom organization and lesson planning that can strengthen and amplify what you already do. Our model, *The Arch of Collaborative, Conversation-Based Instruction,* shows teachers how to enact these research-based standards in a unified system where the whole is greater than the sum of its parts. This pedagogical framework moves us from simply teaching discrete pieces of information toward instruction that encourages active engagement in a lifelong process of self-motivated inquiry.

The Importance of K–12 Through Higher Education Partnership in Teacher Professional Learning

So often, educators in higher education are accused of living in an "ivory tower" without a real understanding of how things operate in schools. There is frequently a disconnect between the research-based practices education

Figure P.2. Theory of Action: K–12/Higher Education Partnership in Teacher Professional Learning

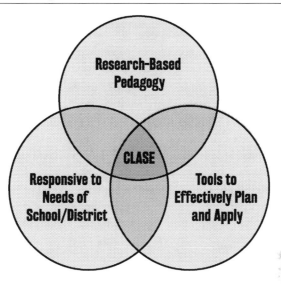

scholars develop and real classrooms. One can have the best pedagogy in the world, but if it doesn't apply to real classrooms, it is useless. Furthermore, while preservice instruction and inservice professional development initiatives may introduce research-based practice to teachers, and teachers may see the value in a practice and fundamentally agree that it is good, they often hit a wall when trying to implement it. Tools for application that can aid in fidelity of implementation are often lacking. But even with both the research and tools necessary, if these are not developed in collaboration with and in response to teacher and district needs, then the practice and tools, however good, will make no practical or substantive change. Therefore, it is vital that researchers and teachers collaborate to develop the tools and skills necessary to effectively and sustainably implement research-based practices that meet student needs (see Figure P.2). These three things—research-based practices, application tools and teacher/district input—must work together in a reciprocal relationship, with each impacting the others, and all working in concert, if we expect to see change in teacher practice.

HOW TO NAVIGATE THIS BOOK

Written as a direct product of the relationship among research, tools for application, and input from the teachers and districts they serve, the purpose of this book is to describe in practical, applied terms how teachers can implement this research-based pedagogy in a systematic way in their classrooms. The outcome goal is to increase collaboration and productive, content-based conversations among all students, thereby improving their linguistic and academic achievement. This book is not a curriculum. In fact, this system can be used with any curriculum because it is not a list of content standards; the tools we outline can be applied at any grade level to whichever standards you are focused on teaching.

Neither is this a "bag of tricks" that comes with an expensive kit and a set of prescriptive, lock-step units one must follow in a predetermined order. Instead, this book outlines a *system* of teaching (symbolized by the Arch of Collaborative, Conversation-Based Instruction; see Figure 1.1) that represents a paradigm shift in how we see the classroom, our students and our role as teachers. We have divided the chapters to mirror the structure of the Arch, with the beginning of the book focused more toward reflecting on the *why*, and the second half of the book focused more on the *how*, offering ideas for practical classroom application of strategies. In keeping with the Arch metaphor, each chapter builds on the previous one and includes the following user-friendly features that enable you, the reader, to extend and apply your learning:

1. ***Notes from the Field***—these vignettes, narrative descriptions with data taken from field interviews and classroom observations, use teachers' and students' voices to show real-world connections and illustrate how the Arch system looks in classrooms. They include questions and opportunities for readers to reflect. We recommend that you take these opportunities to record your thoughts and trace the process of your practice. A journal and pencil icon signals these journaling opportunities.

2. ***Joint Productive Activities (JPAs)***—these focused activities provide opportunities to work in collaboration with your colleagues, practice the theory discussed in the chapter, and employ tools for practical application. These can be done individually, but are designed to be completed collaboratively in groups and to generate rich conversation about the topics discussed in the section in which they appear. If you are working with a team of teachers or a professional learning community (PLC), take 20 minutes or so to complete each activity and then debrief as a group. These activities are designed to provide an applied introduction to Joint Productive Activities (JPAs), the keystone of the Arch system, which are described in Chapter 6.

3. ***Food for Thought***—these quotes and questions invite readers to reflect on these theories and practices, and how they connect to their own life experiences. Readers are encouraged to write about these reflections in their journal, or share with their book study or professional development colleagues. One Food for Thought has already appeared in this chapter and readers may want to use it as a first entry in journaling reflections and application ideas as they proceed through the book.

In Chapters 1 and 2, we discuss the importance of collaboration and conversation and the need for a safe classroom environment (the foundation, in terms of the Arch). Chapter 3 is dedicated to identifying and discussing the importance of the assets that both students and teachers bring to the classroom (columns). Chapter 4 is dedicated to the scaffolding tools needed to support the action (scaffolding). Lastly, Chapters 5 and 6 are dedicated to moving from identifying the potential energy contained in the assets to how to activate the assets, planning with them in mind and using them to meet instructional goals (voussoirs and keystone). Throughout the book we will use many terms and acronyms to anchor the pedagogy. To clarify these terms, we have included a Glossary on our webpage (coe.uga.edu/directory/latino-achievement), which describes how we use these terms compared to how they have been used historically or are used in other approaches.

By "building the Arch" from foundation to keystone, the approach of this book challenges us to reflect on our classroom environment, the assets we and our students bring to the classroom, and the way we plan and support our students' learning, and offers tools for lesson planning and implementation. When applied with fidelity and consistency, this system provides students with rich and challenging opportunities to engage in complex, collaborative conversations, practice language, and think deeply about content.

CHAPTER 1

Introduction

WHY CONVERSATION AS A MEANS OF INSTRUCTION?

The focus of instruction in a collaborative, conversation-based pedagogy must be how to converse productively. But before we can begin to unpack the *how*, it is important that we consider *why* conversation is pivotal to the success of this system. Think about the last time you had a truly engaging, thought-provoking conversation—one that made you think and challenged you to see things in a different way. What were the earmarks of that conversation? What made it happen? How often does that happen in your work, school, home? What needs to happen in order to have more conversations like that? What are the benefits of conversation and collaboration, particularly in the classroom?

Conversation Offers a Space for Formative Assessment

Teachers often point out that collaborative, conversation-based instruction provides opportunities to formatively assess their students in a low stakes environment. The opportunities for formative assessment are particularly strong during what we call Instructional Conversations (ICs), where the teacher is present to facilitate small-group instruction (which we will describe in detail in Chapter 6). While direct instruction is important for introducing new concepts, it can be very difficult to accurately assess what each of your students knows or doesn't know, simply because the size of the group and the dynamics don't allow for it. Imagine that you are teaching a unit on character traits, a 3rd-grade English language arts standard. You are standing at the front of the room, reviewing the list of different traits such as responsibility, perseverance, determination, etc. In an effort to ground the lesson and connect the vocabulary to what the students have been learning, you create a T-chart with the students, asking them for evidence drawn from the informational text your class is reading, to support the claim that Frederick Douglass was "determined." All the students listen quietly and respond when you ask them for evidence from the text; however, there are

1

two or three students who don't speak at all. They appear to pay attention, but it's hard to tell if the quiet ones are actually following the lesson, if they fully understand the concepts, or if they are thinking about what they are going to have for lunch. The point is, if you don't hear from them, it's very difficult to know what they know and to check for misconceptions or places where they might have gaps in understanding. Furthermore, those students who always talk and who come up with the "right" answer may not have really thought out why the answer is correct and may not have a strong conceptual understanding. This is difficult to probe in a whole-group setting where you may not have the opportunity to hear students' reasoning.

Now imagine that same lesson, but rather than working with the whole group and choosing students one at a time to respond individually, you pose the question, "What evidence is there in the text that Frederick Douglass was determined?" but tell your students to talk with the other students at their table to find the answers. You can sit with the group that you are most concerned about (maybe the quiet ones who weren't responding before) to hear their logic and thought processes. You can see where they are struggling and where they are succeeding. Students are able to learn from each other's thinking and build off their peers' ideas. Additionally, you can hear from more than one at a time and use what you learn to adjust your teaching, so that when it comes time for summative assessments, neither you nor your students will be surprised. This kind of activity forms the basis of a good Joint Productive Activity (JPA) that requires collaborative conversation to succeed. The key to a good conversation is creating a complex problem, one that doesn't have a single right answer or a single way to arrive at an answer (we'll discuss that in depth in Chapters 5 and 6).

Collaborative Conversation-Based Instruction has Positive Impacts on Writing

Teachers often share their excitement with the enhancement of student writing through the collaborative conversation process. They remark that when students engage in collaborative conversations, they go on to write about content in a more succinct, yet complex and detailed way, even when the collaborative task was not specifically writing focused. As Billings and Roberts (2014) posit, thinking should be taught as a fundamental literacy skill regardless of the subject being taught. "There is no question that reading, writing, speaking, and listening are interconnected skills that develop synergistically . . . [T]he more fluent students become as readers, writers, speakers, and listeners, the clearer, more coherent, and more flexible their thinking will become" (p. 33). This is one reason why Speaking & Listening

Standards are included with the other literacy standards and don't stand alone. Therefore, it should not be surprising that, though the basis of our pedagogy is oral language use, if students are given tasks where they can talk about their thinking and work through to defend their mental processing with their peers, they are better able to produce clear, well-supported written work.

Let's go back to the example of the character traits lesson. Imagine each small group of four to six students is given a piece of chart paper and asked to talk together to create a T-chart, listing on the left side the character traits that Frederick Douglass demonstrated and on the right side the evidence from the text. The groups then work together to find examples and write them down. They might even write an opening and concluding sentence together. This collaboratively crafted artifact can then be used as a graphic organizer for a follow-up individual writing assignment. Having talked through the evidence and defended their claims, as well as discussed ways to put them into writing, the students go into the writing task with more confidence and clarity about what they will write and why. This illustrates again that while collaborative conversation is not the only productive means of instruction in the classroom, it provides an archway linking direct instruction to individually produced summative work.

Utilizing Collaborative Conversation-Based Instruction Fosters Student Autonomy

There is definitely a place for whole-group direct instruction, that is, introducing a new topic or teaching a mini-lesson before center-based activities. But the teacher doesn't always need to be the hardest-working person in the classroom. So often teachers leave school exhausted, and one reason is that they are doing most of the thinking and talking. In such cases, the teacher is actively working, dispensing knowledge; but the students, while they might be actively listening, are still mostly passively receiving this bundle of information. Also, as we mentioned before, a teacher who is doing all the talking has little opportunity to discover what the students are thinking. These interactions generally follow an Initiation, Response, Evaluation (IRE) pattern: The teacher asks a question and calls on Susie, while the other students wait with their hands up, not really listening to what Susie says, but waiting for the chance to answer (or waiting with their gaze down, hoping they won't be called upon). After Susie answers, the teacher evaluates her answer and then Susie can stop listening for a while, knowing that she will not likely be called on to talk again any time soon. Here, student interaction is almost entirely teacher-directed, where students depend on the teacher to tell them what to do next. This becomes particularly problematic if there is ever an interruption (which so often happens in classrooms).

Intentionally designed, collaborative, conversation-based lessons open spaces for students to work with each other rather than only with you. By providing ample and varied opportunities for students to engage in conversation to solve a problem or to collaboratively wrangle with an idea, the students begin to teach each other. They take more ownership of their learning, becoming more self-directed and confident. The teacher is no longer the keeper of all the knowledge, doling out information to the students one at a time and judging their individual responses.

Furthermore, because this center-based, small-group instruction allows multiple groups of students to be working at the same time, engaging about academic content in a conversational manner, the teacher multiplies opportunities for students to talk and practice, increasing the amount of time that the students can talk through, process, and connect to content during class. As a positive byproduct, students begin to practice and apply social and emotional skills; they become less likely to act out and get off task because they become more confident, self-regulatory, and autonomous in their learning. Given the tools to collaborate and converse, students know what to do without having to wait for the teacher to tell them. Conversation around structured questions and the application of critical thinking to contextualized, content-based problems allows students to take agency over their own learning and to learn from and teach each other. This multiplies and enhances teaching time.

Conversation Provides Authentic, Low Stakes Opportunities for Students to Practice Language

Speaking in class is often risky business. When speaking aloud, not only are students asked to display their knowledge for evaluation by the teacher, they are asked to do so in front of their peers. This can create a very threatening position for many students, particularly for English learners (ELs) and students who speak non-standard varieties, thereby raising students' *affective filter* (Krashen, 1985). The higher their affective filter, the more reluctant students may be to speak in class for fear of making mistakes; this creates a vicious cycle.

Students need to practice language to get good at it, but if their rare opportunities to speak are filled with risk, they will likely avoid even those few chances to talk. If they don't practice language, their language development could slow, which could result in their falling further and further behind, and potentially feeling ever more anxious about speaking in class.

See the pattern here? However, when offered the opportunity to address, in small-group conversations with their peers, the same questions that they were asked to answer in front of the whole group, students have the chance to practice language in a low stakes environment that doesn't require their speaking alone in front of everyone.

Collaborative conversations provide a space for the students to practice their use of language and explore their ideas, increasing the likelihood of their responding confidently and successfully to a similar question in a higher-stakes environment. As a result of interacting collaboratively in the small group, students may feel better prepared and able to take a risk to engage when the stakes are high (Lantolf, 2011; Long, 2014).

Collaboration Focused on Authentic Applied Problems Provides the Opportunity for Peers to Scaffold for Each Other

When students engage in conversation with their peers, they teach *each other*. We have countless anecdotes from students who say that they "learn from their peers" and that they love conversation-based lessons because it gives them the opportunity to "be the teacher." As mentioned before, this collaborative conversation-based learning environment gives students agency. They don't have to wait for the teacher to tell them what to do, because they have the tools to work autonomously and can rely on themselves and their peers to move forward (we'll discuss these tools for scaffolding at length in Chapters 4 and 5). Some teachers express the fear that when students work together, they will teach each other mistakes. However, that fear is not supported by evidence (Lightbown & Spada, 2013). In fact, when students are given the conversational tools necessary to collaborate effectively, they are likely to activate each other's background knowledge, interpret errors, and productively struggle toward not only an "answer" but an *understanding of the concept* and how best to arrive at a solution. The conversation pushes them not only to state what they think and believe but to defend their answers with reasons and support from texts, as well as from personal and shared experience. This skill of articulating their thinking allows students to not only hear themselves and their own thought processes, but to also hear the flaws and holes in others' reasoning and help to identify and correct them (Donato, 1994; Swain & Watanabe, 2012).

Confirming research that peer support builds confidence and facilitates learning (Hudson & Bruckman, 2002), students in classrooms where collaborative, conversation-based lessons are regularly implemented often tell us they like this pedagogy because they get to "become" the teacher while learning from their peers.

Collaborative Conversation Benefits and Facilitates Both Metacognitive and Language Development

John Hattie's meta-analysis (see Hattie & Donoghue, 2016) on different instructional practices shows that collaboration and discussion have the largest effect sizes for the acquisition of deeper learning. Given space that encourages them to engage in conversation, students have the opportunity to listen to others, ask questions, verbalize their thoughts, as well as connect and extend what they know, thereby consolidating their understanding to deeper levels. As Hattie and Donoghue so eloquently state, "It is through such listening and speaking about their learning that students and teachers realize what they do deeply know, what they do not know and where they are struggling to find relations and extensions" (p. 7). Conversation allows the group to synthesize the knowledge of each of the participating students (as well as what the teacher contributes) into a greater whole. As one 5th-grade student says: "Instructional Conversations allow me to think outside my head and learn from my peers" (D. Roberts, personal communication, April 15, 2015).

While the students propel the conversation and the problem-solving, the teacher's role in this process remains vital and generative. By crafting problems that don't have a single right answer or only one way to arrive at an answer, the teacher is ensuring that the students must work through various language and conceptual options and possibilities. This requires both linguistic and cognitive practice. English learners are rarely provided with the opportunity to practice academic language in an authentic context (see Callahan, 2005). But when given regular opportunities to converse with a group of peers to solve problems that have clear instructional goals, students can practice basic communication skills, as well as academic and discipline-specific language, more frequently and with greater levels of complexity, to consolidate their learning and strengthen their language fluency. This requires explicit processing and has a heavy cognitive load. However, the more practice they get, the more authentic and automatic their language use becomes (Swain, Brooks, & Tocalli-Beller, 2002).

Conversation Creates Empathy and Boosts Social-Emotional Learning

Sherry Turkle, a researcher from MIT who studies the relationship between humans and technology, shows that the more technology people use, particularly in handheld devices, texting and emailing, the less conversation they have. What is more alarming is that we are beginning to not be able to distinguish between connection and conversation. We tend to believe that by being "connected" we are somehow doing the work of conversation; however, this is not the case (Turkle, 2017). Conversation has a lot of ancillary benefits in the social construction of community that we take for granted. By conversing, we can begin to build our social–emotional skills—seeing others' points of view and empathizing with them even if we don't agree with them. Turkle states that young people are now 60% less likely to feel empathy for their peers, or to be able to read and interpret facial cues and gestures, than they were 20 years ago, and attributes that to the small amount of conversation they engage in (Turkle, 2017). That is to say, the more that we text and email, the less we talk and the less we are willing and able to talk with and relate to other people.

Conversing implies a certain vulnerability, because you don't know where the conversation is going to go. People are more likely to tackle uncomfortable and difficult situations through texts or email than face to face, because when we talk to someone we must deal with their reactions in real time. But there is a solution: Create more opportunities for conversation. Turkle's work shows that very little conversation is necessary to turn the tide. By engaging in conversation, people begin to understand one another. (We discuss in more depth the connection between collaborative, conversation-based instruction and social–emotional learning—SEL—in Chapters 2 and 4.)

Conversation Supports Listening and Speaking Skills

Why should we, as educators, focus our energies on conversation? These days in schools when teachers have to get through so much material and to teach so many skills, it may seem that the last thing we have time for is talk. However, there are pragmatic, as well as pedagogical and cognitive, reasons why using conversation as a means of instruction is a good idea. Speaking and listening are two of the four modes of language and work in tandem with reading and writing. For this reason, most schools have adopted a set of speaking and listening skills or benchmarks (identified, for example, as standards or "can do" descriptors, etc.) that they require their students to meet (e.g., the Common Core Speaking and Listening Standards, the WIDA Standards, the Common European Framework, etc.). These skills focus on what students are expected to be able to accomplish in terms of comprehension and collaboration, as well as the presentation of knowledge and ideas through oral language use. It is important to underscore that, unlike other subject areas (e.g., math, ELA, science, social studies, etc.) that rely on *individual* ability to demonstrate content knowledge, one must practice interacting with others in order to develop speaking and listening skills and as a result be able to successfully participate in a productive conversation with other people.

Because speaking and listening skills can (and arguably should) be integrated and practiced within all subject areas, they encourage and facilitate academic learning across the curricula, while creating spaces for these skills to be transferred in an authentic way. Educators must begin to incorporate these skills in the younger grades so that students leave school able to interact with a wide audience and to express their ideas with clarity, using evidence and reasoning logically. We cannot afford to ignore these skills in our lessons if we want to produce college- and career-ready citizens who can work together with diverse stakeholders to solve complex, real-world problems.

But even if our only goal were to comply with these skill standards because they are required, the question would remain: How do we teach all the content that we have to teach while simultaneously creating opportunities for our students to collaboratively converse? How do we teach in a way that supports language and cognitive development? We have to change the way we teach so that students are doing more of the talking.

Pinball vs. Ping-Pong Metaphor

Talking in class matters, because how much students talk is correlated with their achievement. One study found that in high-achieving classrooms, teachers talked about 55% of the time, but in classrooms in which students were identified as low achieving, teacher talk consumed a whopping 80% of the instructional minutes (Flanders, 1970). This is striking in light of a more recent large-scale study of elementary classrooms, which reported that 91% of instructional minutes were devoted to whole-class teaching or individual work, with "few opportunities [for students] to learn in small groups, to improve analytical skills, or to interact extensively with teachers" (Pianta, Belsky, Vandergrift, Houts, & Morrison, 2008, p. 1796). When students aren't asked to talk and think, well-meaning teachers fill the time with their own speaking. That's not to say that listening is devoid of thinking, but rather that talking through concepts and problem-solving collaboratively facilitates understanding. When teachers dominate the talk, they—not the students—are doing most of the thinking.

Most teaching in contemporary classrooms looks much like a ping-pong match. It falls within the IRE pattern (Initiation, Response, Evaluation): The teacher asks a question (usually one with a pretty clear answer, e.g., What is the capital of Guatemala?), the students raise their hands, the teacher chooses one student to answer, the student responds, and the teacher evaluates the response. This pattern continues with the teacher doing most

---

FOOD FOR THOUGHT

Consider this quote and how it might apply to your students.

> "It is impossible for someone to learn what they think they already know."
> Epictetus

Growth depends on openness to learning and changing, but you can't grow if you believe you have nothing left to learn. Progress can only be made if we believe we don't have all the answers.

As we move through this text, we ask that you consider that what you "know" to be "true" could be:

- only one of many possibilities
- further enhanced by what others know
- a misconception

With that in mind, we challenge you to:

- choose to have a "beginner's mind," actively looking for new ways of seeing a problem
- be comfortable with being wrong
- ask questions—don't be afraid to look like an amateur
- recognize that focus on *process* leads to mastery

Questions to Consider

Think of a time when something you believed to be true was challenged and you changed your mind. Then write your reflections on the following questions in your journal:

- How did this experience open spaces for new ideas?
- How did changing your ideas impact your relationship to others?
- How does being open to new ideas promote growth and change?
- Why is it important for teachers to have a "beginner's mind"?

---

of the talking and each student speaking only as much as it takes to give these limited responses. Not only do the answers generally not require a lot of higher-order thinking, they rarely open the opportunity for a great deal of language use; once a student has responded, and independent of whether the answer is "right" or "wrong," they know that they are free to relax for a while as the teacher will make the rounds of the other students before circling back to them. Unlike traditional IRE, Joint Productive Activities (JPAs) require that students dive into a question and "trouble" it.

FOOD FOR THOUGHT

Consider the following questions.

As we discuss the components of an actual arch structure, look at the graphic of the Arch of Collaborative Conversation-Based Instruction (Figure 1.1)

- What do you notice about the different components?
- How is the student side different from the teacher side? How is it the same?
- How are your assets different from or similar to your students'?
- What do you need to know about your own assets in order to help your students access theirs?
- What is necessary for the arch structure to stand as you are building it?

Because these activities are based on complex problems that don't have simple answers and require collaborative interaction to solve them, they change the way that teachers and students interact. Rather than ping-ponging back and forth from teacher to student one at a time, the teacher throws a complex question out to the group, like releasing a ball into a pinball machine, and then watches, waits, and listens as the students bounce the idea back and forth amongst themselves. By asking the group a thorny question, one that doesn't have a single right answer or that might require some thoughtful puzzling out, and then allowing the students the space and opportunity to talk through the problem, the teacher becomes the facilitator of the lesson with the students doing most of the talking (and work). The students practice using content-specific language and think through the resolution process critically rather than relying on simple recall. This process takes intentional planning and practice to put in place. However, once collaborative conversation is integrated into your instruction, you and your students can reap the many benefits.

Obviously, changing this paradigm for teaching and learning isn't something that happens overnight or without support. One thing that we have learned through our years of developing this systematic approach to teaching content through applied, problem-based conversations is that both students and teachers need guidance on how to converse in an academic setting. While traditional school models follow the "ping-pong" or "sage on the stage" model, students are not encouraged (much less taught) how to interact with one another, in particular to converse purposefully on academic content. Furthermore, instructional practice is most often comprised

of teacher-led, teacher–student interaction. With that in mind, we will outline tools teachers need to help plan complex, student-centered, culturally
responsive lessons, and tools students can use to collaborate and converse
with one another in a respectful and productive way.

THE ARCH OF COLLABORATIVE, CONVERSATION-BASED INSTRUCTION

To illustrate our system for integrating collaborative, conversation-based
instruction into your classroom, we have developed the metaphor of an
arch. In the following chapters, we "construct" the Arch and describe the
component parts of the structure one at a time. Each of the parts represents
a key idea or process that, when integrated with the others into a structural
whole, forms a classroom system of instruction designed to recognize, access, and take full advantage of the assets both teachers and students bring
to the classroom. When built, the intentional, integrated Arch system is
stronger than the sum of its parts.

The use of construction as a metaphor isn't new; in fact, Aristotle refer-
enced the process of house building when describing his philosophy of the
process of teaching and learning. He said that, like house building, teaching
and learning are both knowledge- and purpose-driven: You have to know
what you are teaching, but you also need to know *why and how* (Bröchner,
2009). Therefore, it seems logical as we begin to ponder how best to convey
the philosophy behind this system of instructional practice, which uses collaborative conversation as its "keystone," that we reflect on the metaphor of
construction and particularly on that of the arch to describe the what, why,
and how of collaborative, conversation-based instruction.

Before you begin to build any arch structure you must consider the location where you are building it (on a mountain? in a plain? in the desert?);
how the arch will be used (will it support a bridge that spans a gorge or an
aqueduct that transports thousands of gallons of water?); and the ground
on which it is to be built (sand, bedrock, silt, or clay?). All these things impact the materials you choose to use and the structure of the arch itself. The
builder has to consider the purpose of the structure in every step of production when choosing tools and materials. Similarly, when you teach, it isn't
enough to just know the content standards you are teaching, you must also
consider the unique strengths and resources your students bring to the classroom that you can build upon. For your students to learn, you must consider what they already come knowing, what matters to them, and how they
might meaningfully apply what they are learning to their lives. These elements must be systematically and intentionally integrated into your lessons

(see Chapters 3 and 5 for concrete examples and practical strategies). Only in this way will what you are teaching land with your students and create a lasting Arch of conceptual understanding.

The construction of an arch depends on the interdependence of its parts; the integrity of the structure depends on the balance and strength of all its components. First and foremost, the arch must be built on a strong *Foundation*. If we are thinking of this arch as a metaphor for collaborative, conversation-based instruction, this foundation represents a classroom environment that cultivates trust, and fosters the intellectual and emotional safety of the whole classroom community. On this foundation, the first blocks of the arch itself are the *Columns* of strength that hold it up. The columns provide the grounding and height necessary to make the arch useful and viable. In the Arch of Collaborative, Conversation-Based Instruction, the blocks in the columns are the assets that teachers and students bring with them. They include the background knowledge, language(s), motivations, and skills of every person in the classroom.

"Springing" from the columns are the *Voussoirs* (the wedge-shaped building blocks in the curves of the arch between the crown and the columns). This is where the action happens—where the Five Standards for Effective Pedagogy are brought to life in the classroom. In the construction of an actual arch, these blocks are where there is both tension and movement. They are not square, but wedge-shaped, so they must be shaped with care so they will hold together and support one another. In the metaphoric Arch, this is where the teacher and students work with language, productively struggle, and purposefully converse to solve challenging and contextualized activities. The word *voussoir* comes from an old French word meaning "to turn." This is where we take what the students and teachers already know, turn it, and work with it collectively to reach from one side of the arch to the other. In the Arch System for Collaborative, Conversation-Based Instruction, the teachers plan lessons that inspire student interaction, the students work to make connections, and the teachers respond by modifying their lessons, thereby deepening the complexity of the learning. In this reciprocal, recursive process, the students and the teachers, like the voussoirs, press against one another in tension and support. Neither can construct the arch by stacking their blocks straight up, building a taller and taller column (even if this means building on the strengths of their assets). For the arch structure to stand, both the teachers and students must change, "turning" toward one another—and through this turning, the two columns (the teacher assets and the student assets) come together to form the arch.

However, to support the stones and prevent them from falling as an arch is being constructed, the builder uses *Scaffolding*. Similarly, as the

Figure 1.1. The Arch of Collaborative, Conversation-Based Instruction

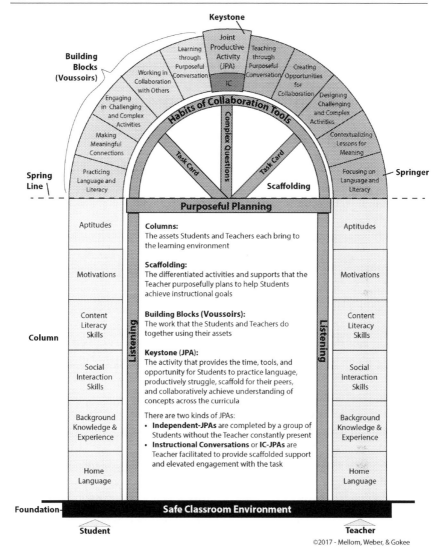

©2017 - Mellom, Weber, & Gokee

teacher begins to enact collaborative conversations in his or her classroom, he or she must intentionally use scaffolding strategies that allow for differentiated instruction. This scaffolding is comprised of complex questioning, active listening that informs purposeful planning, task cards, and other habits of collaboration that include the elements necessary for the instructional system to function effectively. These elements include a center-based classroom, goal-setting, conversation norms, grouping considerations, sentence starters, and teacher conversational moves. Without these elements, the building blocks would fall and the system would not stand as a viable structure.

Finally, what holds the arch structure in place and gives it structural integrity and lasting power is the *Keystone*—the triangular wedge that sits at the arch's apex. When the keystone is placed, the pressure pushes back onto the voussoirs, and the arch stands, creating a gateway from one room, space, or world to another. The keystone in our system for Collaborative, Conversation-Based Instruction is the Joint Productive Activity (JPA)—where students collaborate to solve a problem or produce a product.

The practice described by the Arch of Collaborative, Conversation-Based Instruction challenges our students to wrestle with complex ideas, contextualize content for meaning and relevance, and develop language and literacy skills in all four of the domains (speaking, listening, reading, and writing). It creates a gateway for our students to pass through from the world of their home language, culture, and background knowledge (what they know from home and their life experience) to the world of school language and content knowledge.

It is important to note that each of the arch's component parts are strong and could be arranged independently or in other structures. Collaborative conversations need not be in JPAs to be useful. Good teachers constantly strive to challenge their students and contextualize their lessons whether they are utilizing whole-group, small-group, or direct instruction. But there is great power in the keystone. To extend the metaphor a bit further, arches have been built in dozens of civilizations across the world and have sustained colonnades, aqueducts, and bridges, while also providing openings from one world to another. Just as these physical arches hold things up and provide gateways connecting people and ideas, so does the Arch system for Collaborative, Conversation-Based Instruction. This *integrated system* creates critical supports and gateways for all students, but particularly for the most vulnerable. By contextualizing content and including language and literacy goals in each lesson across the curricula, teachers open cognitive, linguistic, and social doorways for their students, allowing them to pass through into spaces that they might not otherwise have been able to access.

CHAPTER 2

Laying the Foundation
Creating a Safe Classroom Environment

The *Foundation* of the Arch represents the safe classroom environment that must be established for this system to be successful (see Figure 1.1). Like in any building, if you don't build on a solid foundation, the structure will not be stable, will not stand, and will not last. Similarly, if teachers don't establish a classroom community grounded in trust and respect, we cannot expect students to feel safe enough to engage in productive conversations. Before moving through this chapter, consider for a moment the following questions:

- What do people need to feel safe in a community (family, church, school, etc.)?
- What do students need in order to feel safe to take intellectual and social risks in the classroom?
- What can teachers do to promote a safe classroom environment?
- What can we do to build trust among our students?

THE AFFECTIVE FILTER AND ITS IMPORTANCE IN THE CLASSROOM

In the early 1980s Stephen Krashen developed the *affective filter hypothesis* (published in *The Input Hypothesis*, 1985). The *affective filter* describes a psychological barrier that researchers have observed in learners, which makes it harder for them to think. Krashen posited that a high affective filter (e.g., when a learner is nervous, anxious, or under stress) disturbs concentration and makes learning more difficult. For example, EL students who feel that they are at risk of ridicule or who are uncomfortable in class will have a high affective filter and will not comprehend or produce as well as they otherwise might in their first language, much less their second (or third or fourth).

It is common for students, and particularly culturally and linguistically diverse learners, to feel very vulnerable in the classroom. They may be afraid of looking foolish, of being made fun of, or of making mistakes. The more fearful they are, the higher their affective filter is, and the less likely they are to speak and the more likely they are to make mistakes when they do. The key is to create a classroom environment that lowers that affective filter. How can teachers create a safe classroom environment, where students feel safe to take risks and make mistakes and where they don't fear the ridicule or ostracism of their peers or the judgment of their teachers? The norm-setting exercises discussed below will go a long way toward creating that environment.

CREATING NORMS FOR COLLABORATIVE CONVERSATIONS

Even when students are willing to risk talking about content in class, despite fears of saying the "wrong" answer or being ridiculed by their peers (or even the teacher), they may not know *how* to talk with one another about content or to collaborate productively. Therefore, even if you have a great lesson that *should* require the students to work together and talk, we have found, through our own experience and interviews with teachers, that you cannot just say to your students: "Here's the problem—okay, talk!" If you did, you would more than likely be met with blank stares or, at best, one or two students would talk and the rest would sit quietly, nodding their heads in silent agreement. Therefore, one of the key components of collaborative talk is creating an environment that establishes trust between the teacher and the students and among the students themselves. This entails building a shared structure that supports conversation: a collaboratively determined set of conventions for classroom discourse. This is not a top-down, imposed list of rules, but instead a collectively generated and agreed-upon set of standards for how the class communicates. Through these shared norms, students are able to engage in academic conversations and have the opportunity to practice and learn how to interact with one another while simultaneously developing critical social–emotional skills such as self-regulation, teamwork, social interaction, perspective taking, and respect for others. Teachers tell us again and again that these social–emotional skills transfer beyond the walls of the classroom—into the lunchroom, the media center, the playground, and even the home. When teachers give students the tools to talk with one another in a collaborative, productive way, they are supplying tools for success not only in the classroom, but also in society at large.

With this in mind, before we begin any class or professional development, whether we are working with K–12 students, university students, or teachers, we ask the participants to establish a set of norms for collaborative interaction. You may be saying, "We already do this. I have my classroom

---

FOOD FOR THOUGHT

Consider the following. Write your reflections in your journal.

Imagine that you are in Paris. You don't speak French, and you need to find the nearest train station. You approach a Parisian (who doesn't speak English) to ask for directions. You are in no hurry and although you don't speak the language, you feel comfortable asking this individual because they are helpful and willing to work with you to figure out what you need and get you to the station.

   Now imagine how your interaction with this person would be different if you were frightened, frustrated, or worried because you had to catch the train to the airport and you only had 3 hours before your flight was scheduled to leave.

   Imagine if the Parisian laughed at you, got angry with you, or just completely ignored you because of your "terrible French."

Questions to Consider

- How would this impact your ability to speak and communicate?
- What does this tell us about the Affective Filter and its effects?

---

rules hanging up on my wall from the first day." But there are two key differences between classroom rules and the conversational norms we advocate for successful collaborative conversations: (1) conversational norms are not dictated by you, the teacher, but developed and established *in collaboration with your students*; and (2) conversational norms aren't just behavioral "don'ts"—they are about what individuals need to do to make collaborative interaction productive and respectful.

   This means that students must not only think about what they don't want others to do, but also reflect on what they and others need to do to create a safe, productive learning environment. You have to take the time to ask your students what they think are the most important things good listeners and good speakers do, and what they think is necessary for a good class. What norms or group practices are necessary to create a safe space for a productive exchange of ideas? How must teachers and students treat one another in order to collectively work toward shared goals?

   Perhaps not surprisingly, both young students and adults have the same fears. Even very young students have a clear idea of what makes them nervous about speaking in class and what shuts them down. When asked how listeners should behave, a group of 3rd-graders responded with such answers as: look at the speaker, listen carefully, don't get distracted, pay attention to what others say, don't interrupt, disagree respectfully, don't name-call. Recently, we taught a university class and were startled to find that the undergraduates said very similar things: Be present and show that you are listening, don't talk over one another, don't shut others down, agree with one thing the other person says before you disagree, don't be sarcastic, be open to others' ideas, and don't "check out."

When establishing conversation norms that will promote positive collaborative interactions, whether in a kindergarten or university classroom, it is important that the group take those "don't" statements rooted in anxiety and turn them into "do" statements that represent our commitment to positive interactions. So "don't interrupt" might become "allow others to complete their thoughts," and "don't get distracted" might translate into the norm, "be present." The result of collaboratively developing these norms is that the group begins to establish itself as a place of trust and risk-free interaction.

At the core of this is the cultivation of a willingness to be vulnerable within the confines of a safe environment that we, as teacher facilitators, must rigorously monitor. The teacher must engage in close listening throughout the lesson to ensure that even subtle (often unintentional) hurtful comments do not go unaddressed, and that the group is continuously reminded of its norms. Students are often unaware of the impact of their words. Learning empathy and self-regulation is a process. Attention should be directed to the norms before every collaborative lesson and during lessons, when needed. This may take the form of asking students to reflect on the norms and choose one that they want to focus on that day (e.g., I will listen to understand, not to respond), or calling attention to a specific norm when the group has begun to violate it (e.g., reminding the group that has digressed into talking over one another that one of their norms is to allow others to complete their thoughts).

We must also remember that the norms are a living document and can be changed in response to group needs or the dynamics of the classroom throughout the year. The norms at the beginning of the year may not look like those at the end of the year. You may find that at the beginning of the year your class's norms are straightforward, but later they become more nuanced because your classroom dynamics have changed. For example, you may have new students come in, or your students may have developed a deeper understanding of working collaboratively. Revisiting the norms on a regular basis, particularly when something causes them to break down, is an essential component of the process. Revisiting doesn't necessarily mean changing, but a constant engagement with the norms is vital.

Teachers must prove to students the value of productive disagreement as we provide them with the means to productively disagree. Successful

Collaborative, Conversation-Based Instruction depends on the establishment of an environment where each student (and the teacher) is willing to recognize his or her limitations, as well as understand that others' perspectives are valuable, and that it's okay to be wrong. Good collaborative conversation requires that you go into the interaction with a *beginner's mind*—the recognition that your views and understandings will be changed (refined, adjusted, adapted) because only in this way can the group reach consensus and create a collectively agreed-upon product. Creative solutions (and cognitive development) grow best out of active and lively respectful disagreement. To better prepare for this dynamic process, it is critical that time be devoted to collectively creating and establishing norms.

But how does one establish norms to promote collaborative conversations in the classroom that go beyond behavioral norms (e.g., "keep your hands to yourself") or procedural norms (e.g., "silence when the lights are off"), and that don't fundamentally work against collaboration and conversation (e.g., "raise your hand before speaking")? Much work has been done on the importance of establishing norms for conversation (see Johnson & Johnson, 2009; Zwiers & Crawford, 2011)—and not just in education. Michael Schudson (1997) suggests that the problem-solving conversations that foster democratic life (which differ from strictly social conversations) are norm-governed and marked by civility rather than spontaneity. In this sense, norms make civil discourse possible and lay the foundation for productive problem-solving.

We believe in the importance of norms in creating safe classrooms that foster social–emotional learning and promote civil discourse. Drawing from language across disciplines and through the work with our teachers, we have created a table (Table 2.1) sorting norms that promote collaborative conversations into four categories you might consider as you begin to establish your conversation norms with your class. For example, "assume goodwill" is a common norm and is a good place to start to ensure positive, productive collaboration. This norm encourages students to ask questions to clarify understanding, rather than reacting emotionally. Setting norms for seeking clarification in a respectful way, while stating your own opinions and thoughts, is essential to laying the foundation for productive collaborative conversations.

As you open spaces for conversation and develop complex lessons that have multiple solutions, it becomes essential that you establish norms that allow for productive conversations. The types of norms we have listed in Table 2.1 are just a starting point to begin the collaborative process of norm-setting with your group. They should be negotiated with your group, opening a discussion about what your group will commit to and why.

Table 2.1. Types of Norms for Collaborative Conversations

Type of Norms	Characteristics
Norms for a Safe Environment*	• Humility—Be self-reflective and recognize that one's view has limitations. • Empathy—Try to see ideas from another's perspective. • Respect—Make a conscious effort to treat others with consideration, courtesy, and dignity. • Curiosity—Be open to new ideas and actively inquire into other's viewpoints. *This category adapted specifically from Zwiers & Crawford, 2011*
Norms for Speaking (S) and Listening (L)	• Eyes—on the speaker (when L) and on the audience (when S). • Ears—attuned to others' voices (L) and to affirmations, disagreements, and evidence (S). • Mouth—not interrupting (L) and clear and succinct (S). • Body—facing the group (L & S), nodding to show understanding or signal to indicate a lack of understanding (L) and gesturing appropriately to enhance communication (S).
Norms for Collaborative Conversations	• Reciprocity—Everyone participates. • Inclusivity—Recognize that all voices matter and actively invite others' thoughts. • Listening—Listen deeply for understanding rather than to reply or rebut. • Building—Synthesize others' ideas. • Questioning—Clarify and probe for deeper understanding. • Paraphrasing—Restate to check for shared understanding.
Norms for Controversial Conversations	• Confirmation—Check for understanding first, before responding. • Objectivity—Focus on ideas, not people, when expressing disagreement. Frame it as a debate, rather than a conflict. • Community—Actively work to reach understanding, find common ground, and focus on shared goals. One way to do this is to acknowledge where you agree with your critics and what you've learned from them. • Productive Struggle—Be willing to disagree and challenge ideas to learn, not to win. • Flexibility—Be willing to change position or stance when evidence presents itself. Argue as if you're right but listen as if you're wrong. • Generosity—Assume goodwill; make the most respectful interpretation of the other person's perspective.

NOTES FROM THE FIELD

As you read, consider the following questions.

- What strikes you as interesting or surprising about what the students say (and how they say it)?
- How is the connection between social-emotional learning and academic learning illustrated by what these students are saying? Can you give examples?
- What would be necessary to establish in order to make these conversations possible?

In our work with teachers and districts we are often invited to come in and observe classrooms. One day last spring we were visiting Ms. Mueller's 3rd-grade classroom. It's clear from the moment that you walk into Ms. Mueller's classroom that her students are engaged, excited about learning, and focused on their tasks. There is an atmosphere of calm and a clear rapport among students and between the students and their teacher. The day we went to visit, the class was in center time and Ms. Mueller had pulled a group of four students to work with her in an Instructional Conversation Joint Productive Activity (IC-JPA).

The instructional goal of this math lesson was to ascertain the difference between area and perimeter. The sorting task was to discuss different word problems and to collaboratively decide whether they required the operation for determining area or perimeter. The lesson itself sponsored great conversations and allowed for the four students in the group to wrangle with the tricky concepts and revealed some misconceptions. But what interested us the most as we watched was the way the students interacted. Throughout the lesson, they used their conversation norms—disagreeing respectfully, listening actively, adding on to each other's reasoning, and supporting each other's individual conversation goals (see Chapter 4 for a more detailed description of conversation goals).

At the end of the lesson, we interviewed the four, heterogeneously grouped students: Tana, a quiet girl who had been reluctant to participate in class at all until becoming involved in IC-JPAs; Christy, a student who struggled with connecting conceptual knowledge, particularly in math; Katia, a voluble and affable EL who excelled in social language but needed support in academic language; and Katherine, a high-achieving math student who had initially not collaborated well in groups. We wanted to hear their thoughts on how they felt about this kind of lesson. We have transcribed a section of this conversation below.

NOTES FROM THE FIELD, CONTINUED

Paula: How do you feel working in a group like this compared to when you're working by yourself or in the whole class?

Tana: It feels different because usually I'm just all quiet and I don't speak that much and like I'm nervous to talk in front of the class.

Paula: Does this make you feel less nervous? Or not?

Tana: Yes, sometimes it makes me feel less nervous because I get to practice speaking, like pretend that Katia, Christy, and Katherine are the whole class and they are listening to me and I get to feel more confident about myself.

Paula: Ah—alright—How does that make you guys feel? [*addressing the group*]

Christy: It makes me feel more safe.

Katia: Also, I know that she's nervous and I love to like encourage her because that's one of her goals—to like speak more—and when she jumps up, I'm one of the people to like encourage her and like tell her that she has it and she knows like what the answer to the question is.

Paula: What about the rest of you? How do you feel about this kind of activity?

Katherine: I like this group because, maybe sometimes I might get it wrong like I feel nervous if I'm getting it wrong, but then I feel more confident because I know that they are going to back me up and that they are going to help me a little more.

As you establish norms with your class, it is important to remember that norms for politeness—socially accepted behavior that helps people cooperate with others—are culturally bound (Eelen, 2001; Leech, 1983). Groups and cultures vary tremendously as to what is considered "polite" or "respectful." The norm-setting process is further complicated by tension between mainstream norms and the diverse norms for interaction that teachers and our students bring to the classroom. We often assume a common understanding of what polite behavior looks, feels, and sounds like. But as teachers with students in our classroom from different backgrounds, cultures, and experiences, we cannot make these assumptions. Therefore it is vital, as we strive for a safe environment, that we establish, and commit to, basic shared expectations for how to work collaboratively and respectfully toward collective goals in the classroom. Discussing different ideas of what respectful behavior looks like isn't easy and can engender strong feelings. However, it is essential for the academic and professional success of our students that we consciously unpack those norms that often go unexamined.

JPA TASK CARD: NORM SETTING

Instructional Goal(s)

- To collaboratively determine what norms are necessary for successful collaboration.
- To activate thinking for utilizing collaborative norms in your classrooms.

Task Activities

- With your group, brainstorm a set of norms.
- Divide the sheet into two columns.
- On one side of the sheet, make a list of things (behaviors, words, etc.) that have shut you down in previous professional development activities.
- On the other side of the sheet, make a list of norms that we will agree upon to help prevent negative interactions and promote positive, collaborative conversations that will allow us to reach shared solutions to complex problems.

Questions to Consider

- How can norm-setting be used in different settings (i.e., for faculty Professional Learning Communities, grade-level teams, families, etc.)?
- Why is it important to develop norms with each group collaboratively?
- How does developing shared norms increase agency, empathy, self-regulation, student buy-in?
- Why is it important to revisit these norms regularly?

Through this process, students can gain greater awareness of the impacts of their and others' behaviors and, through that understanding, become more self-reflective and more self-regulatory. So, rather than simply being punitive in our approach to "inappropriate" behaviors, collaborative norm-setting helps our students to discuss, reflect upon, and choose for themselves those norms necessary for the positive and productive participation of all students. By taking the time to discuss openly and explicitly with our students what our collectively agreed upon norms "look like," we go a long way toward creating real dialogue and enacting change.

THE IMPORTANCE OF TEACHING SOCIAL–EMOTIONAL SKILLS IN FACILITATING ACADEMIC ENGAGEMENT

Often we think of "behavior" and "academics" as two different things, and think we need to *control* behavior in order to *enable* academics. But what if we recognized that increased social–emotional learning such as self-awareness, self-management, social awareness, relationship skills, and responsible decision making (see www.casel.org) can foster content learning and that the teaching of social–emotional skills can be embedded in how we teach academics? Creating this recognition is one of the critical roles of the Arch System for Collaborative, Conversation-Based Instruction.

There are educators who believe that teachers should not have to waste academic time teaching students how to interact appropriately with each other and that they do not have the luxury of time to create a block of instruction only for these skills. However, many teachers are also facing lost instructional time due to breakdowns in shared norms for positive and productive classroom behavior. The beauty of the Arch System for Collaborative, Conversation-Based Instruction is that you don't need to carve out extra time, because you are actively planning for and teaching the social skills necessary for success *while* teaching the content standards.

Additionally, rather than these being skills that you *hope* will one day transfer to the real world, students are learning, practicing, and applying them to their everyday classroom activities and to their real world, now. School personnel often recount stories about students who are "respectfully disagreeing" as to whose turn it is to play with the ball on the playground, and parents wondering how their child learned to voice her or his opinion so articulately and respectfully. Teachers tell us that engaging students in collaborative, conversation-based instruction changes the culture of their classrooms, and principals assert that it changes the culture of their schools—and this all happens while teaching math, reading, writing, science, and social studies.

Laying a sound foundation that makes it possible to develop social–emotional skills while learning complex content takes time, but that time is well spent, because once the safe environment is established you can move faster and with more assurance that your students are actually learning. With this foundation, your students can delve more deeply into the content because they feel safe taking the risks that allow them to access their assets and make the real connections that are the basis of deep and transfer learning. In the next chapter, as we discuss the columns of strength built on the foundation, we will outline the assets that both teachers and students bring to the classroom, and how we can begin to recognize, reflect on, and access them to promote learning.

CHAPTER 3

Building the Columns

Accessing and Capitalizing on Teachers' and Students' Assets

The *Columns* in the Arch are the pillars of strength that will support the final structure of the Arch of Collaborative, Conversation-Based Instruction. These are the assets that the students and teachers each bring to the classroom. Before we move through this chapter, consider for a moment the following questions:

- What strengths do teachers and students bring to the classroom in the form of their language(s), experience, interaction skills, content knowledge, motivations, and aptitudes?
- How can teachers reflect on their own strengths and recognize, promote, and take advantage of their students' assets?
- How can we build on those assets to enhance instruction?

REFRAMING OUR OUTLOOK: FUNDS OF KNOWLEDGE ARE ASSETS NOT DEFICITS

It is important to remember that students come into classrooms with a lifetime of experience. We often hear others (and sometimes even catch ourselves) focusing on what they *don't* have rather than reflecting on what they do. Everyone has a certain amount of ethnocentrism; people tend to think that their way is the best or, sometimes, the only way. The consequences of these attitudes play out in schools. When students do not present skills and experience that educators take for granted, we may see holes that need to be filled. These deficits could be based on language (the student doesn't speak any or much Standard American English upon arriving at school); knowledge (perhaps the student's family is not a reading family and so she comes to school with little knowledge of how to hold or use a book); or culture (the students' parents don't understand the school system because the processes they are familiar with are different). While it may be true that they don't know what educators know, or what we want them to know, our students know all kinds of things. They don't come to school empty—they haven't been asleep for the last 10 years! When we only consider what students don't have when compared to those in the majority culture—what we think of as normal—educators overlook what they *do* have, which is what they bring with them in terms of home language(s), experience, and background knowledge from such environments as work, home, and places of worship. Luis Moll and his colleagues have termed these assets *Funds of Knowledge*. Moll, Amanti, Neff, and González (1992) argue that these funds of knowledge offer our students a wealth of strengths that we as educators can take advantage of to help them navigate and make meaning of the academic and social terrain that seems normal to us, but is new to them. However, the assets that they bring with them are useless if we do not recognize and access them. We need to use their assets to get our students where we want them to go.

Look for a moment at the Arch (Figure 1.1). As you can see, both the student and the teacher columns are essential to the overall integrity of the Arch structure, and the assets on each side are equally important. This structure cannot stand without everyone's voice, engagement, and commitment to reflection and change, to provide a space for academic growth. We must access both teachers' and students' assets to create a sound structure and help our students to apprentice into the cultural norms of school.

If we don't help our students access these assets, we run the risk of compromising the integrity of the whole Arch structure. Students must access and activate all the assets in their column. If teachers ignore or devalue any one of these assets, students are left with a gaping hole in the column, while the block representing that asset, which is necessary to build the Arch structure, is left lying to the side, disconnected and gathering moss. If we do not listen and plan so that students can access and connect to their assets, it will be much harder for them to bridge the gap between what they know and what we want them to know and to move from their culturally embedded knowledge to the academically challenging concepts we are trying to teach them.

The assets that teachers and students bring to the classroom, the blocks in the columns, are strong and shaped through experience, but we have to learn what these assets are in order to be able to take advantage of them. In order to see clearly what our students bring, teachers must reflect on their own strengths and what they know and bring to the classroom. This process of self-reflection enables us to identify what we see as normal and then, in turn, to identify our students' different strengths through observation and listening. So what are the assets we all bring to the classroom? They are the parallel blocks of the student and teacher columns: home language, background knowledge and experience, social interaction skills, content literacy skills, motivation, and aptitudes.

HOME LANGUAGE

As we begin to think about the assets people bring to the classroom, perhaps the one that is closest to the foundation on which all the other assets are built is home language. People's home language is integral to their selves, connects them to family and friends, and creates a frame for how they see and describe the world.

Everyone comes into the classroom with their own home language—this may be a language other than English, such as Spanish, Vietnamese, or Swahili, or it may be a regional or cultural variety of English, or even the Standard American English we strive to teach in schools. The home language is often at the heart of identity. However, those whose home language is Standard American English have the advantage of being able to speak their home language at school without having to switch or choose between languages in order to be successful in the language of school. Multilingual people whose home language is different from the language of school often reflect that although they can talk about math, science, and history in the language of school, they can more easily talk about the things closest to their hearts (food, family, and feelings) in the language they learned beginning in infancy from their parents, siblings, and extended family. It is not coincidental that we refer to our home language as our mother tongue.

However, when a student's home language differs from the language of school, it becomes more complicated for them to access and utilize this asset. We as teachers must create explicit and intentional bridges between our students' home languages and the language they need to be successful in school. As teachers, we can never be experts in all our students' home languages (and we don't have to be, because they are); however, we are

---

FOOD FOR THOUGHT

Consider this quote and how it might apply to you and your students.

"In order to succeed, I had to stop talking like the people I came from and who I loved and start talking like those that never thought I'd amount to anything."
Elementary School Teacher from rural Georgia

FOOD FOR THOUGHT

To help us access and take advantage of our students' home language as an asset, it may be beneficial to reflect on and become more conscious of our own. Consider for a moment the following questions. You may want to choose one or two that resonate with you and reflect on them more deeply and with specific detail in your journal.

- What does the term "home language" mean to you?
- How is your home language different from the language you use at school? At church? On social media?
- Do you ever consciously switch from one language or "kind of talking" to another? When and why?
- Do your languages ever conflict? How?
- How does our language define or shape our identities?
- Have you ever been in a place where you were the only one speaking your language or variety of language, and suddenly you heard the voice of someone speaking your language? How did that feel?

---

experts in our own home language, whether or not that is the language of school. We, as teachers, have to reflect on and become more aware of our own home language and how it connects us to our lives, experience, and identity, and shapes the way we think; we can then better facilitate our students' metalinguistic awareness of their home language, as well as their new language(s), and encourage them to value and capitalize on them with intention and agency.

This process requires that we think of *all* language as an asset and actively teach metalinguistic connections so that the students' language strengths can be accessed and utilized to increase content understanding. In schools, we often think of students' home language as being a distraction from understanding and a detriment to learning Standard American English and English-based content. However, by treating our students' home language as irrelevant or useless to learning, we run the risk of both dismissing what makes them unique and neglecting one of their most fundamental and influential assets.

Every person's home language—how they learned to talk through interaction with their family and friends—helps shape who they are. Therefore, it is essential that we value and make space for our students' home language in schools; not just because it is inextricably bound with their identities, but also because it can be harnessed to shape language and cognitive development. The skills and understandings that are developed in the first language

---

JPA Task Card: Experiences with Language

Instructional Goal

To raise awareness of the Teacher Asset of home language, and how that awareness can provide a window into our students' home language and the role it might play in instruction.

Task Activities

Consider a moment in your life when you felt embarrassed or made uncomfortable by the way you speak.

- Describe this moment in your PLC. Be specific in your description of what happened; who was involved; how they reacted; what you did in response.
- After you have each described your experiences, synthesize what was common and/or different among each of your experiences.

Questions to Consider

- How do you think your experiences with your home language differ from or parallel that of your students?
- How can you use these experiences to help you tap into your students' home language asset?
- How can we value our own and others' home language(s) and activate them for instructional purposes?

---

can be transferred to help students learn in their second language, and thereby to access and understand content in English. By actively incorporating our students' home language into our instruction, we not only value who they are (which is essential to their sense of belonging and success in school), but we also facilitate their content learning and mastery of the language of school. We will discuss at length explicit strategies for how to activate and incorporate students' home language in Chapter 5. In the meantime, the JPA activity "Experiences with Language" offers you the opportunity to reflect on how your personal experiences with language can provide a window into your students' home language assets and what that might mean for instruction.

FOOD FOR THOUGHT

Consider this quote and how it might apply to your students.

"Contexts make meaning that activates students' learning process." Dalton, 2008, p. 136

Questions to Consider
- What does context mean to you?
- How does context help us learn?
- Think about a time that you felt really engaged in learning.

BACKGROUND KNOWLEDGE AND EXPERIENCE

After home language, the next block in the columns is the background knowledge and experience that all people bring with them. Like home language, much of people's background knowledge is framed by contexts and experiences built at home through interactions with families and friends. These experiences—which can include interactions at home, at work, in the community, at places of worship—help to make sense of the world. They give context to understanding, and that context, and the language associated with it, frames and interprets new experiences. It is not random that this block is laid on top of home language, because home language is the basis for describing experience. Broadly speaking, this means that words take their meaning from the context in which they are found. However, this also means that even if people use the same words, their background knowledge and experience may drive them to interpret their meaning in different ways.

Words and structures are embedded with or void of meaning depending on where you are speaking (and with whom). Even if we are "speaking the same language," there are many culturally and contextually based factors that influence how language's meaning is interpreted. To a Spanish speaker from Michigan, the word *invierno*, "winter," conjures up images of snow and ice, but to a Spanish speaker from Costa Rica, *invierno* is the rainy season. In fact, even though there is a word for "autumn" in Spanish, there is no immediate contextual basis for students in Central America to understand the word the way English speakers in North America generally do. In Central America, there are only two seasons, not four; and though leaves fall, they don't fall in preparation for winter, but instead when it's getting hotter in the summer. The *signifiers* are shared, but the *signifieds* are different. This matters as we plan our lessons.

The problem is that the background knowledge on the teacher side of the Arch is not always the same as that of our students (even when we think that it is or should be). The columns are separated by space and time. Therefore, we must be aware of our own understandings of how the world works—the things we take as givens—and be open to seeing the world through our students' eyes. As teachers, we must be prepared to do more than teach content; we must also offer a view of culture and context as it is applied to this content. This can be surprisingly difficult, as teachers may not be aware how deeply ingrained some cultural frames are—that is, how much we take for granted as just "the way things are done." For example, a teacher might need to instruct students that in America it is not only okay, but expected, to state their claim at the beginning of a rhetorical argument, and that doing so is not insulting to the reader. In some cultures, particularly some Asian cultures, stating your claim too clearly and too soon can be insulting to the reader, implying that you think your reader is incompetent and unable to understand. The ways of framing information can be very different from culture to culture and language to language. Understanding a student's context helps to give us, as teachers, a degree of insight into ways to support the student in skill and content development.

Humans' background knowledge is organized in our minds in contextual frames. Frames are what people use to make sense of experiences and interpret the world. It's how we focus our attention and collectively construct a narrative of what things mean (Kormos, 2014; Tannen, Hamilton, & Schiffrin, 2015). Frames, and other concepts like schemata as developed in both sociocultural and cognitive sciences (see Gass, 2013; Goffman, 1974), can be defined as organized packages of knowledge, beliefs, and patterns of practice that shape experience and allow humans to make sense of their world. Frames aid in the perception, memory, and interpretation of experiences, and are the basis for assumptions about the causes, contexts, and possible outcomes of those experiences. Newkirk and McClure (1992) assert that through activating our frames of experience we "put in place lenses that will help [us] comprehend a story" (p. 100) and through it, our world. According to Scollon and Scollon (1981), people learn from earliest youth how to frame experience through language, how to divide it and categorize it, question it and create it, so as to participate fully in their own culture, society, and family. But those categories or frames are bound by the contexts that each person is familiar with.

As teachers consider what we need to do to make our lessons real, relevant, and attached to what students know, we begin to discover that *we only know what we know*; and, conversely, *we don't know what we don't know*. We each live within our own contextual box, making it hard for us

---

NOTES FROM THE FIELD

As you read, consider the following questions.

- How can we avoid assumptions about what is "common knowl-edge" and unpack our own background knowledge?
- How can we capitalize on our students' background knowledge to make real and relevant connections that help them access content knowledge?

Some years ago, Paula had prepared a simile/metaphor lesson for her 4th-graders. They were reading Jane Yolen's *Owl Moon,* and she had planned her lesson carefully to contextualize the story for them. She knew that be-cause the majority of these young English language learners had been born and raised in tropical countries, they had never seen winter in a temper-ate climate, much less snow. Therefore, she thought that she would have to do some priming to activate their background knowledge, perhaps starting with an introduction to seasons. What she did not take into consideration was that their understanding of seasons was very different from hers—*her box was different from theirs.* So when she began by asking, "How many sea-sons are there?" She was taken aback when they excitedly answered, "Two!" In the tropics there are only two seasons—rainy and dry. This experience underscored for her that what was "common knowledge" for her was not common knowledge for her students and she had to reevaluate what she was teaching and how she was teaching it. If she were to make the content accessible to her students by taking advantage of what they already knew, she needed to learn more about what that was, and not take for granted that they knew what she thought everyone knew and was, therefore, "normal." To collaboratively construct the Arch system, she needed to know about what they knew.

---

to see outside it. We must make an intentional effort to see and understand beyond our own box. The role of teachers should be to strive to recognize our own frames and to step away from them without judging the students' contextual frames, which may be, and often are, quite different. Rather than imposing our frames on our students, we build bridges of real and relevant context for them to cross over, so that they can participate more fully in their new language as a cultural discourse and learn the content we want them to learn framed within contexts that make sense to them. In this way we begin the self-reflection necessary to accomplish the work demanded by the voussoirs: to bend toward one another and meet to create the Arch.

Teachers, in an effort to help their students become socialized into stan-dard linguistic practices and the cultural norms of school and schooling, will make references to popular culture and other common social signposts. However, well-intentioned attempts to connect background knowledge to academic learning often fall flat because what works for students who have the same reference points as the teacher and can make the connections, might not work for linguistically and culturally diverse learners. They simply may not share the same reference points. This often results in our English language learners falling silent as they struggle to understand not only the academic concepts we are trying to convey, but also the "familiar" references we are trying to connect them to. Nonetheless, it is incumbent upon us as educators to recognize that such silences do not mean that our students are blank slates waiting to be written upon, but rather that they are full of competencies that we need to identify and capitalize upon. Practical strategies to recognize and capitalize on our students' assets will be discussed in Chapter 5.

SOCIAL INTERACTION SKILLS

The next block in the columns represents the asset of social interaction skills. Just as background knowledge is built on the block of home language, social interaction skills are built through a combination of the previous two blocks. We learn our social interaction skills through context-embedded, habitual actions within familiar contexts. Much of what we know about how to talk to each other we learn in day-to-day interactions with our families and communities (e.g., taking turns in a conversation, making jokes, greeting peers and elders appropriately, showing camaraderie or deference and respect). However, just as background knowledge varies based on experience and context, the way to interact appropriately varies from group to group, and what's normal in one group isn't necessarily normal in others.

Language Skills *Are* Social Skills

Sociocultural research suggests that language acquisition is fundamentally social (Thorne & Lantolf, 2007). According to this paradigm, social interaction is inextricable from language learning; it not only impacts the thing, it *is* the thing. Therefore, if language is socially constructed, then language and meaning are contextually and culturally bound, and language and meaning are based on who uses it when, where, and for what purposes. These ideas, which have become increasingly influential in social science and education research, are drawn from sociocultural ideas that suggest that *reality is contextual*—appropriated and transformed through historical and social processes.

FOOD FOR THOUGHT

Read these four situations and consider the questions that follow.
1. You are with a group of people and although you have things to say, you feel like you can't "get a word in edgewise" because they are all talking over one another and never seem to stop for breath, much less take turns.
2. You have been trying to get to know a new colleague but despite your every effort to engage, the person responds in one-syllable answers or not at all.
3. You have reprimanded a student in the hallway but rather than looking at you to acknowledge that you have been heard, the student looks at the floor.
4. You are in a meeting and a new colleague comes in late. Rather than simply sitting down, the person interrupts by saying good morning to everyone in the room.

Questions to Consider

- Have you ever been in a situation similar to these? How did it feel?
- Are the people intentionally rude?
- How much do turn-taking practices, politeness, and other social interaction strategies have to do with culture? Social class? Socioeconomic status?
- How do these variations impact classroom culture?
- How can collaborative, conversation-based instruction facilitate the learning of and empathy about differing cultural norms?

The process of language acquisition is much like apprenticing into a language community and becoming accustomed to the linguistic and cultural routines of that community (Lave & Wenger, 1991). How to take turns in conversation, whether or not to look people in the eye to show honesty or respect, and how to greet people are all bound by cultural norms of politeness—norms learned through social interaction with family and social groups. The problem is, teachers might forget that not all people share the same ideas of how to be polite and that what is rude for one group isn't rude for everyone. Our students have learned from their families and communities how to interact in a polite and productive way; however, the norms for social interaction they have learned sometimes conflict with the social interaction norms expected in schools. This creates situations where, in an effort to do what they think is right, students might fall silent when teachers expect them to speak, or speak when teachers expect them to be quiet. And we as teachers, in turn, based on our own frames of social interaction, may

---

FOOD FOR THOUGHT

Consider the following quotes and how they might apply to your students.

"Your assumptions are your windows on the world. Scrub them off every once in awhile, or the light won't come in."
Alan Alda

"Don't make assumptions. Find the courage to ask questions and to express what you really want. Communicate with others as clearly as you can to avoid misunderstandings, sadness, and drama. With just this one agreement, you can completely transform your life."
Don Miguel Ruiz

"People make assumptions and don't take the time to ask about individual experiences. We don't like to admit we don't understand, so we pretend that we do, and our assumptions are often wrong."
Ben Hines

Questions to Consider

- When have you made assumptions that turned out to be inaccurate?
- How do our assumptions about our students and what they know potentially limit how we teach?

---

construct students' silence, apparent rudeness, or lack of understanding as evidence of shyness, limited language proficiency or, in some cases, as their not having the cognitive abilities necessary to be able to grasp the concepts (see Rymes, 2014) when really we have not tapped into what they know in order to understand and utilize it.

When thinking of how these frames for social interaction clash, one might reflect on a first experience in a new setting. For example, a newcomer to the symphony might be embarrassed to find out that, when the orchestra finishes the first movement of a piece, they are among a scattered few clapping in the ensuing silence, not knowing or understanding what is going on or why. The newcomer may know that one claps after a performance to show appreciation, but not know that symphonic movements are framed differently than individual songs. The same thing happens to our students when they try to negotiate the interaction frames of a new language and culture. They are forever clapping into the silence, only to find that what they thought was a sign of respect was, in this new environment, considered boorish. We must guard against making assumptions about why our students are doing what they are doing when it may not initially make sense to us. This is particularly true for linguistically and culturally diverse learners and children of poverty, who may have a much different social interaction repertoire than we have or than is expected in schools.

Basic Interpersonal Communication vs. Academic Language Skills

In leading up to the next block in the columns (content literacy skills), we must first take a moment to introduce Cummins's (1980) concept of BICS and CALP to address its relationship to social interaction skills. Have you ever noticed an EL student whose social interaction skills are excellent—the student's spoken English is terrific; he or she easily goofs around with friends, makes jokes, and can translate for parents—but who has significant difficulty reading and writing in English, particularly on high-stakes assessments? To tease out what teachers often notice as an incongruence in students' communication skills, Cummins coined the terms *Basic Interpersonal Communication Skills* (BICS) and *Cognitive Academic Language Proficiency* (CALP). By distinguishing these two types of language proficiency, Cummins's concepts help us to address and conceptualize this dichotomy.

Cummins used BICS, basic interpersonal communication skills, to describe the language skills necessary to have daily, face-to-face conversations with family and friends, to play on the playground, and to exchange greetings with others on the street or in the elevator. These activities are grounded in social interaction and embedded in regular, familiar contexts with immediate feedback and associative routines that make the interactions more easily negotiated and automatic. Cognitive academic language proficiency (CALP) is more cognitively demanding and less context-embedded than BIC skills (see the section Content Literacy Skills below). Understanding the difference between social interaction skills and content literacy skills, how they are related to one another, and the importance of each, is vital to the success of our efforts to access and activate these assets.

CONTENT LITERACY SKILLS

If Cummins's concept of BICS (which involves mostly speaking and listening) corresponds well with the Arch's block of social interaction skills, his concept of CALP, which covers all four domains of language development (listening, speaking, reading, and writing), maps well onto the next block in the columns, content literacy skills. This block, like the previous block, builds on those before it, but begins to focus on the language and knowledge specific to academic content and the connections between abstract ideas and language. The cognitive academic language necessary for success in school is linguistically and cognitively demanding, in part because it is highly decontextualized and depends on subject-specific language that deals with academic content material. It tends to be abstract, require higher-order thinking (e.g., synthesizing, analyzing, evaluating, etc.), and lacks the benefit of routine, context, gestures, and nonverbal cues. Students trying to become proficient in CALP also rarely have the benefit of negotiated interaction (unless they are involved in collaborative conversation-based activities) to help them learn. So, while the average student takes between 6 months and 2 years of language exposure and use in order to become comfortable and competent in BICS, it can take from 5 to 7 years to become proficient in CALP. Unfortunately, by then, English learners' (and speakers of non-standard varieties of English, as well as children of poverty who face many of the same issues) are often so far behind academically that, even with the acquisition of the academic language, they struggle to adequately catch up with the academic content understanding.

The Arch system is designed to ensure that teachers recognize the different social interaction and content literacy skills that students bring with them, and take advantage of them to create bridges to the new skills we want them to learn. Many of our students come to our schools having been in school elsewhere, whether that be a school down the street or one in a completely different country. Schools in rural areas are often very different from urban schools and curricula and protocols often vary dramatically from district to district and state to state. Although the systems they know and have used may not be the same as those used in our school, the knowledge of how to read in their home language, "do school," and "do math," is transferable. We can take advantage of that knowledge and apply it to how we teach.

Let us not forget that although educators tend to think about academic content knowledge as deriving only from books and schooling, our students, like us, come with knowledge about math, science, social studies, etc., that may not be connected to school-based learning. They may have real-world experience with activities requiring practical application of the concepts we want them to learn. For example, they may know a great deal about geometry and algebra and the mathematical calculations associated with these math concepts because they have worked alongside their parents in construction where they have had to calculate how many boards are needed to construct a shed. Students often have a great deal of experiential applied knowledge, but may not recognize that they know it or have the academic language to access and describe it. Therefore, it becomes incumbent upon us, as educators, to facilitate our students' ability to access this asset by helping them identify what they know from their lives and apply it to

---

FOOD FOR THOUGHT

Consider this quote and how it might apply to your students.

> "Instead of attributing ELLs' failure to their lack of 'academic language,' think about the language demands of specific academic tasks, adjust these tasks as needed for individual students, and provide the type of language instruction needed to accomplish these tasks."
> Wayne E. Wright

Questions to Consider

- Consider what you know about your students and what they come already knowing.
- How can you embed this in your lessons to make them more accessible?

---

what they are learning in school. However, to do this, we must learn about our students and what they know. The more we know about what they know, the better we can teach them.

MOTIVATIONS

The next block in the columns is the asset of motivations. Just as the previous blocks build on the strength of the blocks before them, so does accessing this asset of motivation depend on our activating the assets of home language, background knowledge, social interaction, and content literacy skills. As we access and take advantage of these assets, we increase our students' engagement and interest in what we are teaching. This, in turn, activates and increases their motivation to learn.

Research on motivation in the area of language acquisition has shown that intrinsic motivation is correlated with higher levels of student achievement (Gardner, Masgoret, Tennant, & Mihic, 2004). In fact, Dörnyei and Ushioda (2013) note that in the language classroom, extrinsic motivation (the desire to get an external reward or to avoid punishment, like the promise of a party if you get good grades or the worry that you might not get a good job if you don't learn English) can often negatively impact a student's intrinsic motivation (the desire to learn or achieve for personal satisfaction or accomplishment). Studies show that teacher enthusiasm and behavior can affect motivation. Teachers can bolster intrinsic motivation by implementing practices that increase student engagement (see Patrick, Hisley, &

Kempler, 2000) thereby counteracting the negative impacts posed by extrinsic motivating factors (which we often cannot control). These findings are pivotal, given Hattie's (2008) meta-analysis of research on powerful factors in learning and the role of motivation, as the average impact on achievement can represent more than a year's growth (effect size 0.48).

Recognizing that engagement promotes student motivation, the Arch System for Collaborative, Conversation-Based Instruction uses components that aim to increase student engagement, such as contextualized lessons that incorporate students' funds of knowledge, personal goal-setting that promotes student agency, collaborative activities that encourage student autonomy, and activity design that challenges student thinking, just to name a few. However, these same activities that foster motivation have the potential to negatively impact it because these activities can pose risks, as risk comes with working collaboratively with others on new tasks. Engaging with new content and processes, where there is often the possibility to make mistakes, can be frightening or cause nervousness, especially in front of a student's peers. This risk can be mitigated if there are fewer peers (as is the case when students work in small groups). As students build rapport and establish trust with the other members of the group, they feel more comfortable taking risks, making mistakes, or trying something new.

Teachers can increase and maintain the intrinsic motivation of their students by creating comfortable, stimulating classroom environments that facilitate student participation and student-to-student discourse. When students are given the opportunity to interact and are provided with the tools to do so autonomously, they feel more agency and their intrinsic motivation to learn increases.

NOTES FROM THE FIELD

As you read the following, consider what you know about your students and what motivates them. How can you identify and capitalize on this motivation?

Miguel was one of those kids that every teacher has met. He had a list of "diagnoses" and spent as much time wandering around the classroom from table to table talking to his classmates as he did sitting at his seat focused on his work. He made it hard for others to focus, and the teachers spent countless minutes of teaching time daily telling him to be quiet or sit down. He was a bright and affable boy, but his teachers despaired of finding a way to engage him and help him to focus his attention. Through talking with him and listening to him interact with his peers, Paula found that he had a great love of reptiles and sharks. He had vast knowledge about these animals and could expound at length about them. Once she knew this, to activate his motivation and harness his content literacy skills Paula integrated reptiles and sharks into almost all the content material that she needed him to learn. Miguel became more focused and engaged in the reading because he was motivated by the subject matter. Once he found that he was actually good at reading (and math and science) when he was engaged with things he knew and liked, he became more motivated to tackle material that was less familiar and comfortable. Little by little, Paula was able to wean him off reptiles and sharks and only mention them from time to time to maintain his interest and motivation.

APTITUDES

The last block in the columns represents the asset of aptitudes. Just as we need to consider how to cultivate intrinsic motivation in our students by engaging them in activities that activate and harness their home language, background knowledge, social interaction, and content literacy skills, we need to recognize and capitalize on students' aptitudes so that they might interact more fully in the learning environment. Aptitudes are our innate abilities to do things, either simply because we are born human (as humans are born with the ability to learn language) or because we have individual propensities for something (i.e., "natural" skills in art, sport, or music, etc.). However, when we talk about aptitudes in schools, we tend to focus on tests to measure them (e.g., COGAT, SAT, ACT). This focus can lead us to a limited vision of what aptitude is: These tests don't measure all that we know or are good at. So let's enter the discussion of aptitudes remembering some important qualifications. For one, "natural" aptitudes are not fixed—that is

---

FOOD FOR THOUGHT

Consider this quote and how it might apply to your students.

"Students come to our schools from various walks of life. They have different interests, passions, and perceptions of what is important to them. A focus on developing thinking skills allows all students to take charge of their own learning, deepen their understanding, and become more engaged."
Arina Bokas

Question to Consider

• Consider a moment when you have felt motivated to learn. How did your teacher or the people around you impact that motivation?

---

to say, they can be strengthened and developed (Shenk, 2011). This means that the aptitudes we have can benefit from consistent practice and intentional training. For example, someone like Michael Phelps may have all the right natural abilities to be a good swimmer, but his success is not a product solely of his innate aptitudes, but demanded hours of dedicated and focused practice. Additionally, even if our students don't share our aptitudes, that doesn't mean we can't help them develop theirs.

To take advantage of our students' asset of aptitude and activate it with intention, it is important that we consider what aptitudes we have, at the same time that we inquire into our students' strengths. In this section, we are not going to focus on individual aptitudes (although we encourage you to be self-reflective and help your students reflect as well), but rather we will concentrate on a common aptitude that *all* people are born with and how it applies to language learning.

The human brain is always trying to reduce its cognitive load, and one way it does that is through seeking associative relationships. It is easier for the mind to learn words, concepts, and even grammatical structures if they are connected in pairs, groups, or chunks. This is why mnemonic devices are so useful. Whole generations of students would likely never have remembered the names of all the planets (including poor Pluto), much less in order, had it not been for the mnemonic device "My Very Efficient Mother Just Served Us Nine Pizzas." The human brain has the natural ability to look for things that go together in order to connect and remember information and concepts. Some pairs or groups of words are found together more than their individual frequency would suggest, and therefore, they "predict" each other. In the field of corpus linguistics, pairs of words that frequently occur together are called *collocations*. English has many such combinations (often

---

FOOD FOR THOUGHT

Look at the following groups of adjective/noun pairs. Which ones sound right together (implying that they collocate) and which ones don't?
1. Strong Coffee/Powerful Coffee
2. Tall Tree/High Tree
3. Heavy Rain/Weighty Rain

Questions to Consider

• Why don't synonymous adjectives necessarily collocate with a given noun?
• How can we use what we know about collocations to activate this attribute and facilitate our students' language and concept understanding?
• Are there any common associations that you could make more explicit for your students?

---

adjective/noun combinations such as *densely populated, bated breath, preconceived notions,* etc.).

Similarly, conversation analysts study everyday social interaction and look at what they term *adjacency pairs*: that is, phrases that match up. So, for example, when I meet you in the hallway and say, "Hi, how are you?", there are only a few, predictable ways that you can answer. You might respond with, "Fine, how are you?" or perhaps, "Not so well. My feet really hurt!" But you will not likely answer with, "Unicorns are rare." If you did, it would sound strange and likely cause confusion.

Adjacency pairs and collocations help us in our daily interactions by making it easier for our brains to access language and not work so hard. These predictable pairings allow language learners to acquire language more quickly because the associations allow them to create "semi-preconstructed phrases that constitute single choices" (Hoey, 2012; Sinclair, 1987) or "formulaic sequences" (Wray, 2005; Wray & Bloomer, 2013) that are retrieved from memory as a whole piece, not having to be individually chosen, analyzed, and pieced together.

Like adjacency pairs and collocations, metaphors are another way the brain takes advantage of its aptitude for seeking associative relationships to learn language and make meaning. Metaphors can be both treacherous and advantageous to our students, who come with the cognitive ability to create word associations and will do so. But because they may not have been exposed to the language associations that seem common to us, they might not make what seem to us to be the right ones. Metaphors are culturally

---

JPA Task Card: Jabberwocky

Instructional Goal

To promote reflection on the language learning aptitudes that we have and consider how to activate that through our intentional lesson planning

Task Activities

- Read the first two stanzas of "Jabberwocky" by Lewis Carroll.
- With your colleagues, create a chart indicating the part of speech of each underlined word with evidence for how you know.
- Then, create a detailed description of the Jabberwock. What do we know about the Jabberwock? What is it? Where does it live? Include evidence for how you know.

"Jabberwocky," Lewis Carroll

'Twas brillig and the slithy toves
Did gyre and gimble in the wabe:
All mimsy were the borogoves,
And the mome raths outgrabe.

"Beware the Jabberwock, my son!
The jaws that bite, the claws that catch!
Beware the Jubjub bird, and shun
The frumious Bandersnatch!"

Questions to Consider

- What did you notice about the process of identifying the parts of speech of the words?
- What skills did you intentionally (or not) call upon to understand the words?
- How did you know how to describe the Jabberwock and its habitat?

---

bound, and therefore the associations made in the majority culture might not be obvious to culturally and linguistically diverse learners. This means that teachers must make intentional efforts to raise students' *metalinguistic awareness* of connections and associations so that they can take advantage of this cognitive aptitude. This means making connections not just on the conceptual and contextual level (addressed in detail in Chapter 5) but on the word and grammatical structure level as well. If we are more intentional about calling our students' attention to associative relationships and raising their metalinguistic awareness, we can help them to access and activate their own language aptitudes and go a long way toward promoting their

---

JPA TASK CARD: EXAMINING THE ASSETS

Instructional Goal

To examine what assets teachers and students bring to the classroom environment

Task Activities

As a group, create a three-column chart with the three headings: Student, Assets, Teacher.

- List the Assets from the Columns in the Arch graphic in the center column.
- Provide examples of your assets as a teacher in the left column and your students' assets in the right column.
- Be specific in your description of what you and your students bring to the learning environment.
- Identify the parallels and differences between teacher and student assets.

Questions to Consider

- How are the teacher assets different from the student assets in each block?
- How do they complement one another?
- What does this reveal about what each of us brings to the structure?
- How can we identify, cultivate, and capitalize on our community's assets?
- How does reflecting on our own assets help us to identify and acknowledge our students' assets? How might it create blind spots?

---

understanding and acquisition of language.

For example, the famous Lewis Carroll poem "Jabberwocky" is peppered with nonsense words; nonetheless, when we read it we are able to make meaning from the words based on the associative relationships we have in our minds, our understanding about how words in English go together, and what different word endings mean. Although many of the words do not exist in the English language, we can nevertheless identify them as verbs, nouns, adjectives, and so forth. We can also clearly describe the Jabberwock and where it lives—in spite of the fact that it is a fictitious creature.

When we read this poem with teachers, they often say that they have used both their learned and intuitive understanding of grammar to access meaning. For example, "borogoves" has the article "the" before it so we know that it is likely a noun; and because "gyre" and "gimble" follow the verb "did," they are likely verbs. Teachers also rely on what they know about common forms of words and word patterns. For example, "slithy" is probably an adjective because it sounds a bit like "slimy" and ends in the letter y, as do many adjectives.

So what does this example tell us about how we automatically use our aptitude for language to make meaning? We do this without thinking because we have this natural aptitude; but how much more powerful could it be if we were aware of this skill and used it intentionally—polishing and honing it through practice? How can our understanding of this aptitude help us, as teachers, plan lessons to raise students' metalinguistic awareness and help them access and activate their language learning aptitude? How can our brain's aptitude for seeking and learning through associations be applied to learning academic language and concepts? (See Chapter 5 for practical strategies.)

REVIEWING OUR ASSETS: THE COLUMNS OF STRENGTH

Let's consider again the Arch system with its two supporting columns. Although we might like to believe that we as teachers bring to the learning environment everything necessary for teaching and learning to take place, *both* columns of assets are necessary for the Arch to stand. Remember, one side comprises what the student brings and the other what the teacher brings. As teachers, we must acknowledge that we come in with our own set of assets, and just because these are familiar and may fit seamlessly into the majority culture, they are still only one column in the Arch's supporting system. We must access both our *and* our students' assets to create a sound structure and help our students to apprentice into the cultural norms of school.

The columns, and the assets that comprise them, are essential to the Arch system, but they need to be activated to be useful in the teaching/learning process. We will soon look at how these teacher and student assets can be intentionally harnessed—through planned processes and engaging activities—to practice and learn language and complex content. But before we discuss these processes and activities, we must focus on the scaffolding needed to support them. In the next chapter, we will delve into the tools and supports necessary for teachers to plan effectively, and for students to interact collaboratively and productively.

CHAPTER 4

Framing the Scaffolding
Providing Differentiated Support

As we discussed in the previous chapter, the columns, which represent the strengths of both the teacher and the students, stand apart; they do not meet on their own (see Figure 1.1). They are strong, but they are separate. Therefore, to construct an arch, the wedge-shaped voussoirs that curve toward the apex must be shaped so they will "bend" toward one another, uniting the individual columns into a single, strong structure. Unlike the blocks in the columns, the shaped voussoirs cannot be stacked one on top of the other. Just as the process of accessing and activating each member's assets to create a strong learning environment is tricky business that sometimes takes a leap of faith, laying the voussoirs is equally challenging. The wedge-shaped blocks are heavy, and until all are in place and supporting one another, they will slide off and crash to the ground unless they have a supportive scaffolding underneath them to hold their weight. We can help the process and keep the blocks from falling (and thereby create productive, conversation-based group work that doesn't devolve into chaos or silence) through careful planning and strategically placed support. The *scaffolding* that holds up the collaborative, conversation-based instructional system is grounded firmly on the foundation of a safe classroom environment (see Chapter 1) and comprised of components necessary to plan for and practice language and literacy, contextualize for meaning, maintain rigor, and collaborate productively. In this chapter, we will outline the scaffolding tools we have developed in collaboration with teachers, as well as guidance for how to use them to support productive group work and strengthen learning. We will discuss the five parts of the scaffolding—listening, purposeful planning, task cards, complex questioning, and habits of collaboration tools—describing what each one is, why it's important, and how to use it to support collaborative, conversation-based instruction.

It is important to note here that the tools in the scaffolding are not just pretty laminated kits, tricks, or glossy posters of strategies that one can buy in the store, hang on the wall, and forget about. These tools are paradigm-shifting processes and habits that must be learned, practiced, and consistently used by both teachers and students to create change and allow for collaborative, conversation-based group work in the classroom. It is time consuming and requires individual and group commitment (and work), but it all begins with a willingness to listen to each other.

LISTENING

Supporting the rest of the scaffolding frame, grounded on the foundation of a safe environment, and juxtaposed to the columns and their assets, the scaffolding's primary support posts represent the learned skill of listening. In order to promote collaborative conversations in classrooms, reflect on our individual challenges, and activate our assets so that the group can reach its shared goals, both students and teachers must learn to listen deeply to one another—listen to *understand*, not to respond.

Participating in a conversation isn't just talking. It's also listening to those with whom you are conversing, not creating a one-way transfer of thoughts. Too often people fall into the trap of not really listening to conversation partners, instead spending the time they are talking waiting for them to stop. We all know that listening is important in the classroom, but we tend to think that listening is exclusively the job of the student, and that we, the teacher, need to keep talking. However, listening is just as important (if not more so) for teachers. Listening frames and supports both the student and teacher sides of the arch; both teachers and students must learn to listen in order to build a complex, reciprocal exchange that integrates both parties' ideas into a strong, unified whole.

What is Good Listening?

But what does good listening look like? We know what it feels like to *not* be listened to—to feel that your conversation partner has missed your point entirely, that your words have been twisted or taken the wrong way, or when you are talking with someone and it is clear that they are not listening to what you are saying. And how often are we ourselves guilty of tuning out, or of "hearing" an erroneous version of what someone says because we already "know" what they are going to say and shut our ears rather than listening to understand what they actually say?

Although we know that listening is a key component of collaboration (it is difficult to collaborate with someone if you don't know what they think), few people have a clear understanding of what it takes to ask someone about their thoughts and to listen to, retain, and build on what they tell

---
FOOD FOR THOUGHT

Consider the following scenario.

A few weeks ago, Paula was in choir rehearsal and the director, Stephen, was getting frustrated because the sections weren't blending well: the sopranos were overpowering the altos and the basses weren't in tune with the rest of the choir. Stephen, in an effort to get the singers to listen to one another, moved them all around so that they were no longer in sections, but instead standing next to folks who sang different parts. Each singer really had to pay attention to stay on pitch, come in and cut off on time, and blend well with the group—with no one overpowering anyone else. The exercise reminded Paula that choral singing is like collaborative conversations: Each part, though different, is necessary to make a cohesive, beautifully textured piece of music. However, in order to create that perfect blend of voices, every singer must *listen* to the others to create a balanced harmony where each voice is heard and valued.

Questions to Consider

- What is the value to having multiple voices in a choir? In a conversation?
- How is having a conversation and collaborating with people with differing viewpoints like trying to have a perfectly blended choral ensemble?
- What role does listening play in each?
- How does one balance one's contributions with those of the other choral/conversation partners with none overpowering the others or completely disappearing?
- How does deep listening help us avoid discord?

---

us. As rudimentary as this sounds, research shows that people remember only 25 to 50% of what they hear (Graham, 2006; Headlee, 2017). That means that although speakers hope that they are getting their points across, often very little is being processed or retained by the hearers.

This is because listening (unlike hearing, which is involuntary and effortless) is *hard*. It takes effort, concentration, and a putting aside of self—you have to be willing to stop thinking about what *you* think long enough to try to fully take in and understand what someone else thinks (Stewart, 1983). Like most other skills, this doesn't come naturally; it takes practice. One has to put in the time to get good at it. It helps to have a set of guidelines for how to listen carefully and intentionally with the goal of understanding,

synthesizing, and applying what others say. To support the scaffolding of
the Arch of Collaborative, Conversation-Based Instruction, we have developed a set of principles for active listening drawn primarily from the field
of counseling psychology (Bertolino & O'Hanlon, 2002; Cormier & Hackney, 2015; Hoppe, 2006; Jacobs, Masson, Harvill, & Schimmel, 2011).
These include such principles as: be present, use verbal and nonverbal cues
to show you are listening, clarify with feedback, don't take it personally,
try not to judge, don't interrupt, and reflect and respond according to the
norms. We have found that the same principles developed through research
often turn up early among the norms our student and teacher groups create
for themselves. This underscores that educators already know these principles are critical; we just need to remind ourselves to be intentional and
mindful about enacting them in a habitual way.

Seven Principles and Practices for Deep Listening

1. Be present. Don't allow your mind to wander to the next thing you are
going to say, the grocery list, or the child who just got up to sharpen his pencil . . . again. Give the speaker your undivided attention. In order to be fully
present when you are trying to listen, we also encourage you to put away
your technology. Not only are we not as good as we think at multitasking,
when we try to do two things at once we inadvertently communicate to the
speaker that they are not important enough to receive our full attention.

2. Use both verbal and nonverbal cues to show you are listening. Make sure
that your body is open; lean in and face the speaker rather than looking
away, at your laptop/cellphone, or at someone else. Nod occasionally and
encourage the speaker with verbal comments like "yes" or "uh huh." Don't
be afraid to mirror the speaker's emotions, allowing yourself to feel sad
when they are expressing sadness, or happiness when they are expressing
joy. These cues communicate to the speaker that you are following their
train of thought.

With this principle, we would like to include a couple of caveats:

- Body language is not universally interpreted across cultures and
  groups; therefore, it is important to discuss what your cues mean
  with your students (see the section on creating norms in Chapter 2).
- Even if you are enacting all the nonverbal and verbal listening cues,
  students can tell if you are not truly paying attention.
- Be aware of how your validation is impacting your students; you
  don't want students to look only to you for validating cues and

---

JPA Task Card: Promoting Deep Listening

Instructional Goal

To promote thinking about strategies that encourage students to listen deeply in order to converse collaboratively.

Task Activities

With your professional learning community (PLC) group:

- Discuss the 7 Principles for Deep Listening and determine which are the most challenging; give evidence.
- Sequence them in order of importance for you as teachers.
- Finally, discuss how this order might be different for students.

Questions to Consider

- How does shifting the focus from "being right" or getting the "correct" answer to discovering different perspectives on a problem change our listening habits?
- How do computers, phones, and other "mediating tools" impact (both positively and negatively) our ability to listen and converse productively?
- How can we invite a reluctant partner into the conversation by using our listening tools?
- How can we disagree or challenge an idea without making the other person defensive?
- Which of the principles are the easiest for you? The most challenging?
- What strategies can you identify to help you meet the challenge?

---

forget to listen to each other.

3. Clarify with feedback. Our interpretation of what is said is colored by our own biases, assumptions, beliefs, and filters. These can block our listening and understanding. Remember that the job of a listener is to try to understand what the speaker is saying from their point of view without interpreting their words through our own lens. To do this you can:

- Ask clarifying questions (e.g.,"What do you mean by . . . ?"; "Is this what you mean?")
- Paraphrase (e.g., "What I am hearing you say is . . ."; "I think you mean . . .; is that right?")
- Summarize (e.g., "So, the main points you made were . . .")

It is important to model these practices for your students and talk explicitly about what you are doing and why, so that they can begin intentionally practicing these habits as well. You may want to model for the students how to wait until the speaker pauses before asking a clarifying question like, "Hang on, are you saying that . . ." (see Table 4.1, p. 70 for additional examples). You might also give your students a list of question starters as a scaffolding tool (see Table 4.2, p. 72, for examples).

4. Don't take it personally. Sometimes we find ourselves reacting emotionally or taking someone's comments personally. It is hard to listen to someone when they are saying things that we fundamentally disagree with or that feel like a personal attack. If this happens, rather than bristling or shutting down, it's often helpful to begin by going back to the norms and "assume goodwill." That is, begin with the assumption that the person did not purposefully craft their comment with the intention of hurting your feelings. Take a deep breath and then, going back to Principle 3, ask for clarification. For example:

- "I am not sure I understood what you are trying to say (and I find myself reacting personally to)"
- "I heard you say X, and I interpret that to mean Y. Is that what you meant?"

5. Try not to judge. Listening to understand is not about judging. So, while you are listening, try not to seek the flaws in the argument or to think about your rebuttal. Try to listen with an open mind, as the speaker may have a completely different lived experience from yours or a way of viewing the problem that can open new paths of thinking for you. Remember, the goal is to create *collaboratively derived, mutually agreed upon* solutions to shared problems. This might mean that the best way isn't your way.

6. Don't interrupt. Sometimes it is hard to wait until someone is done speaking without wanting to interject. We might feel excited because we made a connection or afraid that if we don't speak now, we might forget our own point. However, when we interrupt, we risk making others feel their words don't matter. It's important to remember that some people have a hard time getting their thoughts out quickly or concisely—but this doesn't mean they don't have anything to say. Some people process more slowly; others may be trying to juggle multiple language repertoires. Although this can sometimes be frustrating for the listener, if we give each speaker the time to complete their thoughts, they will often say something that helps us think differently, make a connection, or craft a counterpoint. Letting the speaker finish his or her thought without interrupting, even to ask for clarification, allows space for that connection to happen. It also creates that space for each group member, whether or not they are the quickest speaker, to feel heard and valued. On the flip side, speakers need to recognize the importance of relinquishing the floor. If a speaker goes on and on without pause and without inviting others into the conversation, it becomes a monologue, not a dialogue.

7. Reflect and respond according to the norms. We listen actively to gain understanding and perspective, not to win points. Collaborative conversations are based on mutually agreed upon norms for respectful, productive interaction that allow everyone in the group to be heard so shared problems can be addressed. As teachers, we want to model habits of collaboration and create safe spaces for open and civil discourse. This means that we must reflect on what we think *before* we respond. Sometimes we speak before thinking about the impact of our words, as an impulsive response or even just to fill the silence. We truly must remind ourselves and our students of the norms every time we begin in order to promote productive dialogue. This isn't to say that we should not speak our minds, even if we disagree; disagreement is healthy and can lead to greater understanding and positive change. However, it is incumbent upon us to do so in a way that does not shut down conversation and inhibit productive collaboration. If we are diligent in our mindfulness of the norms when the subject of the conversation is mundane, then it will become natural to respond candidly, but respectfully and empathetically, when the topic of the conversation is more controversial.

Good listeners do not just sit quietly, they interact and engage with their conversation partners. How many times have you said something and thought no one was listening or no one really cared because no one said anything in response? Even when we are listening effectively, if we don't respond, by asking questions and connecting to what the speaker is saying, communication and collaboration can break down. When we ask questions, and share the connections we make, we can learn more about one another, empathize more, and further develop our own thoughts. To invite and invoke good listening means to practice and value being a good questioner, summarizer, and connector.

Remember, we are preparing our students for a lifetime of interactions with diverse groups of people who will not always agree with them. By providing them with the tools and time to practice listening, we are equipping them to go into these encounters better able to respond with grace and

JPA Task Card: Summarizing and Synthesizing

Instructional Goal

To promote thinking about strategies for questioning, summarizing, and connecting that promote deep listening.

Task Activities

Take a moment to think of an interesting, scary, or surprising experience you have had on a vacation. Prepare to tell your story to your partner/group using as much detail as possible. Include in your story: Where did you go and why? Who was with you? How did you get there? What did you see and do? When was it? How did you feel?

- Choose one person to begin as the first speaker.
- Setting a timer for 2 minutes, the speaker shares his or her story while the other listens without interruption. (The listener may take notes, if desired.)
- The listener(s) may then ask clarifying questions for 1 minute.
- The listener(s) then summarizes the story back to the speaker, highlighting the who, what, when, where, and how, and makes one connection to the speaker's story (2 minutes).
- The speaker then responds to the connection (1 minute).
- Switch roles and begin again.

Questions to Consider

- How could being completely silent shut down rather than open up collaborative communication? How does it open it up?
- How does having a safe environment impact our and our students' willingness to share?
- How did the turn-taking order change the story you told?
- What does turn-taking look like in a collaborative conversation? How is it different?
- How do asking questions and connecting ideas show we are listening? How might these actions demonstrate the opposite?

prepared to collaborate productively. But to create spaces that encourage listening, we must plan intentionally.

PURPOSEFUL PLANNING

Just as the columns are strong on their own but need to be intentionally joined, the posts in our scaffolding (teacher and student listening) must be intentionally connected. The crossbar of purposeful planning connects the listening posts and supports and influences the remaining components of the Arch scaffolding. For collaborative, conversation-based instruction to be successful, it is essential that teachers plan carefully so that students have the tools and skills necessary to work autonomously in a collaborative, engaged way. This means that much of our work as teachers is front-loaded and happens well before our students ever come into the classroom. This purposeful planning includes all of the remaining scaffolding components specifically designated in the Arch, such as complex questions to engage students in deep thinking, task cards to promote student autonomy, and the habits of collaboration tools that students need to work together effectively. These elements will be detailed later in the chapter; in this section, we will pull out and discuss two other important components that are often taken for granted or overlooked, but that are vital for the system to be successfully implemented. This planning includes creating a classroom that accommodates centers, even in middle and high school where this may be less usual, and grouping intentionally (being flexible and thoughtful to create collaborative groups for your students' different needs).

Setting Up Centers

One of the foundational elements for creating successful conversational collaborations is by creating time and space for centers. Centers allow students to engage, explore, discuss, and investigate concepts that are new to them, while providing students with a safe environment to practice ideas and make connections with things that they already know, as well as with previous experiences. Simultaneously, centers provide teachers the *space* to enrich, reteach, formatively assess, and enhance students' learning, as well as the *time* to listen and get to know students in their classroom so that they can further contextualize and differentiate student learning.

A classroom that accommodates centers, with established routines for how to work independently, and together in groups, is necessary for this system to work because it allows the teacher to focus on one small group while the rest of the class is working autonomously. We recognize that this is a challenge, as is classroom management in general, but we feel strongly that it is a challenge worth addressing and planning for. The loss to impactful instruction is significant if your classroom structure cannot provide a space for small-group center activities, or the classroom management techniques to keep students engaged (see Chapter 6 for examples of different classroom structures and how these might look).

There are many ways to run and plan for centers in your classroom (most primary school classrooms utilize centers in one form or another), but here we mean dividing your class into smaller groups that work simultaneously. Centers can be implemented in all content areas and at all grade levels. We have implemented centers in classrooms from pre-K to university graduate levels and have found them to be an engaging and productive way to multiply teaching time. In centers, the students are all working at the same time on activities meeting their instructional level, applying and practicing the concepts you are teaching, without having to wait for you to assist them—but again, these structures and activities must be *intentionally* planned. Your role as a teacher to formatively assess, clear up misconceptions, bump up the complexity, model language, and deepen conceptual understanding is pivotal.

Intentional Grouping

Approaches to grouping students for instruction vary depending on the instructional goal. For example, the teacher might begin with benchmark assessment data, and group students by those who have mastered the skill and need to be pushed further, those who need more practice to solidify the skill, and those who need to be retaught. You may also determine groups based on who gets pulled out of the classroom for Gifted, Special Education, ESOL services, or EIP support, among others, due to the logistical nightmare that the pull-out schedule provokes. Your instructional goal may mean that you choose to group based on who gets along with whom or who can be counted on to support their peers. We can't tell you the "right" way to group your students, but we would like to encourage you to consider a number of variables such as conversation skills, content knowledge, personalities, behavior challenges, and safe environment needs along with the other factors you use to determine the best grouping to meet your instructional goals. We would also encourage you to be flexible in your grouping over time; that is, be mindful of changes in your instructional goals and change the grouping accordingly.

In order to increase collaborative conversations in a small-group setting (such as a Joint Productive Activity, or JPA), it is important to include students who can provide a language model and conversational support for each other. In addition to considering content instructional goals, below are some of the questions you might want to ask yourself as you plan your groups in order to better develop your students' listening and speaking skills as they deepen their content understanding. While we understand it is impossible to plan for all possible variables at one time (and we are confident that there are additional considerations we have not included here), the following should generate thinking and support your planning:

- Who would benefit from having peers modeling Standard American English? Who might serve as a model?
- Who is quiet and will need encouragement? Who will serve as an encourager, without taking over?
- Who monopolizes the conversation? Who will work well with such students and remind them of the norms and their personal goals?
- Who are friends? Is this a good thing or not in promoting collaborative conversations?
- Who does not get along? Is this an opportunity to work on those relationships, or would it hinder growth?
- Who is a natural leader?
- Who could be a leader with some encouragement? Which students could promote that skill?

Another critical scaffolding tool that builds off the crossbar of purposeful planning and provides support for student learning is the task card. Let's look at how the task card allows us to meet our instructional goal while building student engagement and autonomy.

TASK CARDS

Notice on the Arch diagram that the task card spokes begin at the purposeful planning crossbar and radiate out to support *both* the teacher side and the student side of the Arch. Task cards have two main objectives: (1) to facilitate the teacher's purposeful planning, and (2) to promote student autonomy. Below, we discuss the parts of a JPA task card that provide a framework you can use as you plan (see coe.uga.edu/directory/latino-achievement for task card template and grade-level specific examples). A JPA task card supplies guiding questions to help you as you design your lessons, asking you to: contextualize the lesson; articulate your instructional goals (for both content and language development); identify your task structure; list the materials necessary to complete the task; specify the steps of the task in student-friendly language; include questions to consider while completing the task; develop debrief/reflection questions for after the task; and identify follow-up activities. As you look at the task card components, think about how these parts are similar to or differ from the lesson plans that you currently use.

JPA Task Card Structure and Components

Contextualizing the Lesson: In order to support student learning, it is vital that we connect our lessons to what the students already know. Therefore, the first part of the JPA task card asks you to consider what the students would need to know to be able to participate in this lesson, and to figure out how to activate this knowledge. Think about the lessons you have already taught, what activities your students have participated in, and how this lesson connects to their lives. The following are examples of what you might include in this section in order to connect student learning to their background knowledge and experiences:

- Questions that activate prior knowledge and connect the concept to students' lives and common experiences
- Links to videos/websites/books used to teach the concept
- Vocabulary students need to understand to work on this task
- Anchor charts you've created
- References to previous lessons

Instructional Goal(s): This section is perhaps the most intuitive for teachers because we are constantly thinking about what standards we want to teach. To complete this section of the task card, you might list the verbiage from your school or system's standards alongside a version of the standards rewritten to match the academic level of your students. Include both content and language goals.

Content Goal Example:

- *3rd-Grade Math:* Explain equivalents of fractions through reasoning with visual fraction models. Compare fractions by reasoning about their size.
- *3rd-Grade Student Friendly Math:* I can compare equivalent fractions by their size, using words, pictures, and models.

Consider and purposefully include what language skills or processes you will target with this lesson, being mindful of the four domains of language development (listening, speaking, reading, and writing).

Language Goal Example:

- *3rd-Grade ELA:* Engage effectively in a range of collaborative discussions (one-on-one, groups, and teacher-led) with diverse partners on grade 3 topics and texts, building on others' ideas and expressing their own clearly.
- *3rd-Grade Student Friendly ELA:* I can work together with my peers by adding to what they say through sharing my own ideas.

Although it may seem odd to think of language goals if you are teaching math or science, we stress the importance of purposefully planning for language goals as part of the JPA lesson for several reasons: (1) all students benefit from targeted support in language skills, and for CLD students this support is critical; (2) the processes and skills necessary for language development support content literacy in all subject areas; and (3) different disciplines have different "languages" (including vocabulary, argument structure, genre, etc.), and we must explicitly teach them. (For more ideas about how to incorporate language and literacy across the curricula, see Chapter 5.)

JPA Task Structure: In this section we suggest that you determine and include the structure of the JPA *product* that will be collaboratively produced by the group. It is important, as you design your JPA tasks, that you think about how the task supports your instructional goals. Teachers sometimes lead with the task rather than the instructional goal, and the unfortunate result may be an interesting task that engages the students but fails to accomplish the instructional purpose of the lesson. So, for example, if your instructional goal is to have your students compare and contrast two historical figures, you might choose a Venn diagram as the JPA structure. However, if your instructional goal is that your students determine the character traits of the protagonist of a story, you might choose a T-Chart as the JPA task structure because they can write the traits on one side and cite text evidence on the other (see Chapter 6 for a detailed list of JPA task structures). When you choose the JPA structure, be mindful of how this structure ensures collaboration. Not all activities *require* that students work together to complete them.

Task Materials: In bulleted form, list the specific materials necessary to complete the collaborative task. This list supports student autonomy (and helps you stay organized).

Task Activities: In this section, design a numbered set of clearly stated steps that ensure that students collaborate, discuss (remembering to use their conversational stems), and create a joint product or solve a complex problem relating back to the instructional goal(s). Remember to frame these steps in language appropriate to your students' age and developmental stage. If you are working with CLD students (and particularly ELs), consider including graphics or translations using QR codes that make the instructions accessible to your students.

Questions to Consider: Include two to four higher-order questions that you might ask (or that your students might ask each other) during the task. Such questions require the students to synthesize, evaluate, infer, and apply their learning as they are working through the JPA task at hand. These questions should:

- Enrich the JPA activity;
- Trouble common misconceptions; and
- Move students beyond surface learning using complex thinking.

Debrief/Lesson Reflection: Different from the questions to consider that are part of the lesson, these are questions we ask after the JPA task to ensure that our instructional goals have been met. These questions encourage students to:

- Apply their learning in new and different ways that connect their understanding to other contexts *(Content Debrief)*;
- Reflect on the *process* of the JPA task (e.g., how the collaboration helped them master the instructional goal, how well they met their conversation norms and goals, etc.). When possible, the teacher also gives each student feedback regarding their participation *(Process Reflection)*.

Follow-up Activities: In this section of the task card, suggest one or more follow-up activities for students to engage in once they've completed the JPA task. Consider where this lesson fits in your unit plan and what it leads to. Follow-up activities can be individual or group assignments, can happen either immediately following the task or later in the unit, and could be designed to:

- Build off the knowledge gained during the JPA;
- Transfer student learning to future JPAs/lessons etc. within the unit (for example: "Now that you have learned about fraction models, create a recipe and show how it could be doubled and halved"); and
- Integrate their learning into other subject areas (for example, "Using the knowledge you gained in math about fraction models, write a how-to exemplar for your recipe," or "Design a fraction model showing how the 13 colonies were broken up into the New England, Mid-Atlantic, and Southern Colony Regions").

Lesson Plan vs. Teacher Task Card vs. Student Task Card

Recognizing that the dual purpose of the task card is to support teacher purposeful planning and student autonomy, as you begin to use the task card you may notice that many of the components of the task card are the same as elements you might already include on a lesson plan. For example, your lesson plan probably includes an instructional goal—the content objective or standard that you want the students to learn in this lesson. However, there are other elements of the JPA task card that likely diverge from lesson plans you are familiar with and may seem less intuitive. For example, one may not always think to include language goals on a social studies or science lesson, but they are included on the JPA task card because, as the research shows, having language and literacy objectives regardless of which subject area you are teaching is vital to the facilitating language development of all, but particularly CLD, students (Gibbons, 2009; Lyster, 2017; Walqui, 2006). Furthermore, there are language processes in all four of the language domains (speaking, listening, reading, and writing) that help support conceptual understanding. The task card tool helps you to plan to support the learning of the content by intentionally including language goals in your lesson.

Another difference from a common lesson plan is the inclusion of the task structure. We suggest that this be included because we find that one distinct difference between a JPA and other conversation-based lessons is that JPAs have a clear collaboratively produced product. By having teachers reflect on what that product is and include its structure on the task card, we help to ensure that the lesson is more than a rich discussion. A third major difference from a common lesson plan is that the JPA task card has two sets of questions: those for during the lesson and those for after. Questions asked during the lesson are intended to help the students dive deeper in their thinking and not focus simply on completing the task. The debrief questions are essential to make sure that the students have met the teacher's instructional goal and that common misconceptions have been addressed.

TEACHER JPA TASK CARD EXEMPLAR: WHICH ONE DOESN'T BELONG?

Contextualizing the Lesson

Students have been introduced to the "Which One Doesn't Belong?" JPA and practiced in whole group several times before participating in this activity. This lesson builds on the mini-lesson we did at the beginning of the week on shapes and their different attributes, in addition to several read-aloud books (fiction and nonfiction) about Halloween. Because this lesson was conducted in late October, the pictures I used to compare were of pumpkins—making it more real and relevant because it related to Halloween.

Instructional Goal(s)

Content: 1st-Grade Math Standard

- Distinguish between defining attributes (e.g., triangles are closed and three-sided) versus non-defining attributes (e.g., color, orientation, overall size).
- Build and draw shapes to possess defining attributes.

Language: 1st-Grade Listening and Speaking Standards

- Participate in collaborative conversations with diverse partners about grade 1 topics and texts with peers and adults in small and larger groups.
- Follow agreed-upon rules for discussions (e.g., listening to others with care, speaking one at a time about the topics and texts under discussion).
- Build on others' talk in conversations by responding to the comments of others through multiple exchanges.
- Ask questions to clear up any confusion about the topics and texts under discussion.

Build vocabulary for comparing shapes, for example: *belong, different, same, because, attribute, triangle, circle, square.* (For this task card the teacher also incorporates words that describe chosen photos.) *Pumpkin, seed, stem, pulp, bumps, eye, mouth, nose, big, small, round, orange, green, light, heavy, candle, carved, jack-o-lantern, pumpkin patch.*

We have developed this task card structure in collaboration with teachers and instructional coaches and have found that each of the sections in the task card is critical for helping to ensure that teachers plan lessons that will promote rich conversation, productive collaboration, and a deeper understanding of content concepts.

TEACHER JPA TASK CARD EXEMPLAR: WHICH ONE DOESN'T BELONG?
CONTINUED

JPA Task Structure: Which One Doesn't Belong (WODB)?

Task Materials

Four sets of four pictures for each group of students. The pictures represent pumpkins with different attributes (i.e., different shaped eyes, mouths, and noses). May also include other variations (carved vs. not carved, green vs. orange, stems vs. no stems, etc.) *(Google images "WODB pumpkins" for more ideas.)*

Task Activities

> Step 1: Go over conversational norms with your students.
> Step 2: Ask each member of the group to choose and share their conversational goal.
> Step 3: Choose one set of pumpkin picture cards to match the differentiated needs of your students.
> Step 4: Have students work together to examine and discuss the pictures and decide which one doesn't belong, or go with, the other pictures.
> Step 5: Encourage each student in the group to share their thinking and provide evidence.
> Step 6: Do the same for the other three sets of pictures. [Teacher may include a QR Code, providing an oral reading of the task card.]"

Questions to Consider

- Why do you think those pumpkins (or pumpkin patches) fit together?
- Why do you think that one doesn't belong?
- How could you change the picture that doesn't belong to help it fit in with the other pictures?

Debrief/Lesson Reflection

Content

- What were some of the details you noticed that helped the pictures go together?
- Were there any sets of pictures where you had difficulty deciding which one didn't belong? What made it hard to decide?

TEACHER JPA TASK CARD EXEMPLAR: WHICH ONE DOESN'T BELONG?
CONTINUED

Process

- How did you work as a group?
- Were you respectful and helpful with the conversation norms? Are there any norms we need to add?
- How would you rate yourself in the group?

Follow-up Activities

- Students could use a T-Chart and glue the three pictures from each group that belong together on one side and write their reasons why they go together underneath using the target vocabulary, and then do the same for the one that doesn't belong on the other side of the chart.
- Students could choose one of the sets and then draw another item that either would or would not belong, using details from the set. Encourage use of descriptive language.
- Students could create their own set of cards with other seasonally themed pictures, and share their set with other students.

While the task card is a vital tool for teacher planning, it serves a second and equally important role in promoting student autonomy. When students engage in a JPA, having a task card to guide them increases the likelihood that they will be able to work independently and to delve more deeply into the content on their own. However, you may not be able to just hand your students the task card that you have prepared when you planned the lesson; what is appropriate and necessary for you as you create your task card (the teacher task card) may need to be changed significantly in order to make a task card that is appropriate for, and usable by, your students (student task card). If you teach middle school, the teacher task card may look very similar in both language and content to the task card you give your students to guide them as they engage in the JPA activity. However, if you teach 1st grade, the teacher and student task cards may look dramatically different.

On the following pages, we include an authentic teacher and student task card created by a 1st-grade teacher trained in the Arch system who is also a member of a team selected by their district to support peer teachers in their development and implementation of the collaborative, conversation-based pedagogy in their schools. We invite you to examine the two exemplar JPA task cards (teacher and student for the same JPA lesson), and then with your PLC, complete the JPA that follows (see JPA Task Card:

STUDENT JPA TASK CARD EXEMPLAR: WHICH ONE DOESN'T BELONG?

Instructional Goal(s)

Content: 1st-Grade Math Standard "Can Do" Descriptors

- I can talk about "attributes" of shape, color, position, size, weight, and ways things are the same and different.

Language: 1st-Grade Listening and Speaking "Can Do" Descriptors

- I can listen to others and ask questions about their thinking.
- I can follow our conversational norms and rate my conversation with the group.
- I will learn and use vocabulary such as: *belong, different, same, because, attribute, triangle, circle, square, pumpkin, seed, stem, pulp, bumps, eye, mouth, nose, big, small, round, orange, green, light, heavy, candle, carved, jack-o-lantern, pumpkin patch*

JPA Task Structure

Which One Doesn't Belong (WODB)

Task Materials

Four sets of four pictures for each group of students.

Task Activities

Step 1: Go over conversational norms.
Step 2: Choose and share your individual conversational goals.
Step 3: Take one set of pumpkin pictures.
Step 4: Look at the pictures and decide which one doesn't belong or go with the other pictures. Be sure to share your reasons.
Step 5: Make sure that everyone in the group takes a turn, and shares their thinking about that set of pictures.
Step 6: Do the same for the other three sets of pictures.

Questions to Consider

- Why do you think those (pumpkins, patches) fit in with the others?
- Why do you think that one doesn't belong?
- How could you change the picture that doesn't belong to help it fit in with the other pictures? [Teacher included a QR Code here, providing an oral reading of the task card.]

JPA TASK CARD: EXAMINING TEACHER AND STUDENT TASK CARDS

Instructional Goal

To promote thinking about the differences between a student and teacher task card and how they promote teacher planning and student autonomy during JPAs.

Task Activities

With your PLC:
- Examine and discuss the teacher and student task cards above.
- Create a Venn diagram comparing the student task card and the teacher task card.
- Determine what qualities each should have in order to meet the goals of student autonomy and teacher purposeful planning.
- Give evidence for your decisions.

Questions to Consider

- How do the teacher task card and the student task card support purposeful planning and student autonomy?
- How does the purpose of student autonomy drive the characteristics of the student task card?
- What characteristics do the teacher task card and the student task card share? How do they differ?

Examining Teacher and Student Task Cards). As you look at these examples, consider how using these tools might support purposeful planning and student autonomy.

The JPA task card promotes teacher planning and student autonomy by creating a structure to think about how our instructional goals and the structure of the activities we ask our students to engage in are connected. One key to that connection is the questions we plan.

COMPLEX QUESTIONING

The last spoke of the scaffolding is the central spoke of complex questioning. This spoke directly supports the keystone—the Joint Productive Activity (JPA)—and is essential for collaboration and deep complex thinking. The effectiveness of a JPA to accomplish these goals often hinges on the complexity of the question the students are asked to solve. Questions such as "What year was the Declaration of Independence signed?" might be important for targeting recall of information, but they don't promote discussion

FOOD FOR THOUGHT

Consider the following: While most of us would agree that open questions lead to more complex answers than closed questions, how often have you asked an open question but were listening for one single answer?

Questions to Consider

- How can a closed question become open?
- How can we increase the complexity of thought by troubling our students' assumptions?
- Is there ever a time that you would want to start with closed questions and then move to open questions? Why or why not?
- How do you decide which kind of questions (open or closed) to ask? What about the task informs that decision?

or collaborative interaction, much less critical thinking. Closed questions are good places to start a conversation, check for basic comprehension, and summarize ideas because they sponsor short and often one-word answers, while open questions encourage students to give more information (Christenbury & Kelly, 1983) and promote more complex answers.

Questions that promote productive conversation and deep thinking are those for which there are varying approaches, or multiple answers. JPAs lend themselves to complex problems that provide a space for students to explore varying approaches to reach an answer, while still requiring evidence-based solutions. For example, after checking to make sure the students have a basic understanding about the facts around the Declaration of Independence and when it was signed, you might have your students engage in a JPA that asks them to create a timeline of events that led up to and immediately followed the writing of the Declaration of Independence. You might include questions on your task card such as: "What was the relationship among these events?" This kind of question requires not only knowledge of the events surrounding the event itself, but a more nuanced understanding of how those events impacted one another. This would also promote discussion and spur the consultation of texts and/or the production of an artifact that could then be used as a springboard for writing. As you prepare your questions, consider the common misconceptions your students struggle with. For additional ideas, you might also want to google "common misconceptions" for the concept you are teaching. For example, if your task was for your students to complete a timeline of events surrounding the signing of the Declaration, questions addressing some common misconceptions

---

JPA TASK CARD: CLOSED OR OPEN? THAT IS THE QUESTION

Instructional Goal

To practice creating questions that promote deep discussion and explore how closed and open questions can be layered to scaffold understanding of complex concepts.

Task Activities

- In your PLC, examine these questions.
  - » What is an immigrant?
  - » What is the difference between an immigrant and a refugee?
  - » Why do people immigrate?
  - » What states have the fastest growing immigrant populations?
  - » Would an American who has moved to Costa Rica permanently be called an immigrant? Why? Why not?
- Create a five-column chart and rewrite the questions in column 1.
- Decide as a group if each question is closed or open and write your reasoning in column 2.
- For those you determine to be closed, change them to open questions that would promote more discussion and complex thinking; write your modified question in column 3.
- In column 4, write what instructional goal might be met by each of the questions.
- Lastly, choose at least 4 of the questions from columns 1 and 3 (both the closed and open) and reorder them in column 5 thinking about how each might lead into one of the others; write your reasoning for the order.

Questions to Consider

- When can an open question shut down discussion?
- How can a question with a single right answer still promote reasoned discussion and complex thinking?
- How can we plan a set of interrelated questions to create "cognitive wobble" and productive struggle?

(such as that signing the Declaration of Independence immediately started a war or that it was signed on July 4th) could be posed to promote discussion and deeper understanding.

We are often reluctant to ask a complex question because we can't control where our students may go with it. They may take the question in directions that we had not anticipated and are seemingly off-task, or ones that can be intriguing, but also nerve-wracking. We are therefore tempted

---

NOTES FROM THE FIELD

Consider the following scenario and the questions to consider.

Recently we had the privilege of observing a 1st-grade JPA lesson with four students sorting books into the categories of fiction or nonfiction. The teacher had a large T-Chart on the table with "Fiction" heading one column and "Nonfiction" heading the other. She had selected pairs of books—one fiction and one nonfiction—about the same topic that the students were already familiar with (e.g., *Owls* and *Owl Babies*) and had gone over the characteristics of fiction and nonfiction texts that they had been studying. The JPA task card had directed the students to discuss the books and sort them into the categories of fiction or nonfiction, giving their evidence.

When we arrived, the students were already deeply engaged in the activity. A cinnamon-skinned girl with a bright red bow on the top of her head said, "I think this one is nonfiction," picking up the book entitled *Owls* that had a full color picture of a Great Horned Owl on the cover, "because it has real pictures."

"I respectfully agree with Joanna because it has pictures and it also has a glossary," chirped a round-faced boy with ruddy cheeks and a black long-sleeved T-shirt. He turned the book in his hands and leafed through to the Table of Contents to show the others. The children went on like this for 10 minutes or so, sorting the books, using appropriate academic language as they offered their reasoning for their decisions—clearly demonstrating that they understood the basic text structures and what they meant.

But then the teacher placed a book entitled, *Thomas Jefferson: Life, Liberty and the Pursuit of Everything* on the table. A small girl with straight black hair falling over her shoulders picked up the book and opened it, turned to the front pages, and stated with clear certainty, "I think this one is nonfiction, because it is about a real person."

Joanna, frowning, turned the illustrated cover toward her groupmates. "I respectfully disagree with you, Jesminder. I think this one is fiction because it doesn't have real pictures."

The students continued to go through the list of the text features they knew and were confounded by the fact that the text had some of the features that they were confident belonged to nonfiction texts (i.e., facts about Thomas Jefferson and his house) but others that they associated with fiction texts (i.e., illustrations).

When they had gone back and forth for some time and seemed to have stalled, the teacher asked, "I agree with Joanna—this picture is an illustration, not a real picture, but I'm wondering, can a text have drawings and still be giving us information?"

NOTES FROM THE FIELD, CONTINUED

The students paused and looked at the illustrations, then leafed through the book, looking more carefully at the actual text, discussing whether or not the text was telling a story or just giving information.

Joanna said, "It talks about when the house was built and who lived there."

"I agree," said Jesminder, "but it also talks about how he kept changing it."

Finally, the teacher came back around and asked, "So, do you think this text tells a story or gives us information? How do we know?"

The students finally agreed that the book gave information about Thomas Jefferson rather than telling a story about him and therefore was nonfiction.

By listening to the students' discussion, the teacher was able to identify their misconceptions, and through her questions was able to guide them to a more complex understanding of the difference between fiction and nonfiction texts.

Questions to Consider

- What planning was necessary to promote this kind of collaboration and rich conversation?
- How did the teacher guide the students to discover and arrive on their own at a deeper understanding of the difference between fiction and nonfiction texts without giving them the answers?
- How was the students' understanding made deeper by the teachers' complicating the simple definitions of fiction and nonfiction that they knew?

---

to ask closed questions (that have clear single answers). Learning to ask complex questions isn't easy and takes practice. Just as students need to be taught how to converse, teachers need to be given tools to facilitate complex conversations. When we first started working with teachers in this pedagogy, we found that while they might have every intention and desire to change their interaction patterns with their students, they didn't know how to ask questions to facilitate student interaction. They would either withdraw completely (sometimes because they were afraid of taking control and not letting the students talk, and other times because they couldn't get the students to stop deferring to them) or they would continue to jump in and "save" their students whenever they hit a challenge, often just giving them the answers rather than asking a well-placed question to guide them to their

Table 4.1. Teacher Facilitative Moves

Remember, the best question in the world is useless if it does not respond to the students' needs at that moment. By listening deeply and intentionally to the students' conversations you will better understand what they know and how they think, and thereby be better able to assess what they need to gain a deeper and more complex understanding of the content. This chart offers suggestions for questions you might ask within six themes for what you might want your students to focus on.

Theme	Academic Language	Complexity	Using L1 Assets	Connecting Ideas	Listening	Collaboration
What are you noticing?	You hear the students using "conversational" language to talk about content and you want them to think about when and how to use academic language	You hear the students are responding in a superficial or nonspecific way to the content and you want to promote deeper thinking	You hear the students using their home language and you want to increase their metalinguistic awareness of their home language to support their use of English	You notice that the students are having trouble applying the content and you want to promote their making connections and synthesizing of ideas	You notice that the students are not paying close attention to what their peers say and you want to promote deeper listening	You notice that the students are having trouble collaborating and want to encourage their use of tools (i.e., norms, goals, sentence stems, etc.)
What could you say?	• What's the "school" word for that? • How would you say that if you were talking to a scientist? • How would you explain that same idea if you were a commentator on CNN?	• Tell me more about your thinking. • What evidence do you have for that? • What if X were different? How would that change the outcome? • What can you infer about what will happen next/as a result?	• Is there a word in X that looks or sounds like that word in English? • Do you notice any patterns in these words or structures? How are they different or similar in English and X? • Have you seen parts of these words in other words? • How would you pronounce this word in X? How are those sounds different/similar?	• What connections do you see between these two ideas/books/themes? • What do you think is the main theme that crosses over all these ideas? • Does this idea look like anything we have seen in other places? • That is an interesting idea, how can you connect that to what X said?	• How do you think what X said differs from what Y said? • Can you repeat back what X said in your own words? • How would you paraphrase the idea that X expressed?	• You did a great job building off X's idea. • X's goal is to contribute more, how can you help X meet his/her goal? • Which of the norms should we pay attention to right now?

own process of discovery. Changing behaviors is difficult and requires new tools. Therefore, we developed a set of teacher facilitative moves designed to scaffold ways to ask purposeful questions of students. These questions strive to support better listening, richer student–student interaction, and a deeper and more complex understanding of the content material.

Table 4.1, Teacher Facilitative Moves, divides questions into six themes and then gives prompts for when you might use them. For example, if you hear your students using their home language and would like them to activate this asset by making connections between their home language and English, you might ask, "How is this word/structure in your home language similar to or different from the word in English?" This kind of question allows the students to access their assets and use what they already know as tools they can employ to learn English and content concepts.

This list is by no means exhaustive and is intended to simply get you to begin thinking of the questions that you might ask that could open rather than close conversation and collaboration among your students. These questions can be used in real time in response to observations of what is happening in your classroom (and those are powerful); however, we also recommend that you think about your instructional goal and use the task card tool to *plan* for questions that might come up and that will guide your students as they move through their JPA. Remember that the key is asking questions that will lead to deeper complexity of thought and richer collaboration.

HABITS OF COLLABORATION TOOLS

Just as teachers need tools for questioning, so do students need tools to collaborate and converse productively. At the top of the scaffolding frame is the arc of habits of collaboration tools. This arc rests on the posts of listening, is supported by the crossbar of purposeful planning and the spokes of task cards and complex questioning, and it takes the brunt of the weight of the voussoirs. This arc can only fulfill its task if the habits it represents are consistently and intentionally practiced. In order for students to be able to use the task cards autonomously and work together in groups in a respectful and balanced way, they must develop and strengthen their habits of collaboration tools through mindful reflection and regular use.

Because traditional classroom instruction is teacher-centered, it is rare for students to have regular peer-to-peer interactions. This is especially true for culturally and linguistically diverse learners. As we discussed in the listening section above, even when students are given the opportunity to interact, they are not often actively *taught* how to listen and converse

Table 4.2. Student Sentence Stems for Questioning and Interaction

If you want to:	Ask for more time, or clarification:	Agree and support what was said:	Disagree and share your own ideas:	Agree and build on another's thinking or synthesize ideas:	Disagree but build on another's thinking or synthesize ideas:
Level I	• Could you please repeat that? • I am still thinking about what you said and need a few more minutes to think.	I agree . . . *(and then give evidence from your experience, the text, another lesson, or the world to support your conclusions)*	I (respectfully) disagree because . . . *(and then give evidence from your experience, the text, another lesson, or the world to support your conclusions)*	• I agree with X, and what do you think about this idea? • Your comments have made me think about X. Now I'm thinking Y.	• I know that this idea may be different from yours (or unpopular), but I think . . . • Although I disagree with X you have made me rethink.
Level II	• Tell me more about why you think that? • I'm not sure I understand your point. Would you please explain it to me again? • I'm not sure what that means, could you explain it in this context?	I agree with you because . . . *(and then give new evidence from your experience, the text, another lesson, or the world to support your conclusions)*	I (respectfully) disagree with you because . . . *(and then give new evidence from your experience, the text, another lesson, or the world to support your conclusions)*	• I agree with your idea, and think it's like X *(and then give your idea for how this idea connects to your experience, a text, or another lesson)*	• I hadn't thought about it from this point of view. While I disagree with X part of what you said, I think we both agree that. . . . • I don't think I completely disagree with you, but I want to better understand what you are saying. Could you explain again?
Level III	• How do you know that? • Could you explain your reasoning to me? • How did you come to those conclusions? • When I was reading, I was wondering about X. What do you think?	I agree with you and it also makes me wonder . . . *(and then give your idea for how the answer might be different if certain conditions or elements changed)*	I (respectfully) disagree with you but it makes me wonder . . . *(and then give your idea for how the answer might be different if certain conditions or elements changed)*	• This is like when X so we might try Y. • This reminds me of X except this time Y. • This made me think about work we did in X and it makes me wonder if we might X.	• Although we have differing ideas about how to approach this, I wonder if there are things we can agree on? • Although both these solutions are valid, what is the best way for this situation?

in a respectful, productive, or collaborative way. By giving students tools to listen, respond, and interact with thoughtful comments, questions, and connections, we help them to develop agency in their conversational choices by increasing their metacognitive awareness of what they are doing when they interact.

Sentence Stems

With this in mind, we have developed, in collaboration with teachers, a set of conversation starters, questions, and sentence frames designed to provide scaffolding for students. These tools are important for all students, but are particularly crucial for CLD students, as they give them semi-preconstructed phrases helpful for interacting productively with their peers and others. These stems are divided into five categories that help students to listen deeply, support their thoughts with evidence, synthesize, paraphrase, and evaluate other's ideas. Additionally, we have arranged the stems into three levels of increasing complexity within each category, so that teachers may introduce them in stages (see Table 4.2, Student Sentence Stems for Questioning and Interaction).

We suggest that initially you start with "I agree because . . ." or "I (respectfully) disagree because. . . ." These dichotomous options introduce students to the process and practice of both listening and expressing their thoughts in a simple but robust way. Insisting that the students use "because" ensures that they will have to support their thoughts with evidence and think through their reasoning. It also avoids their falling into the habit of saying "I agree," without really knowing why, and slows down the conversation, providing a space for listening and processing their peers' comments. In addition to these two stems, we also suggest that you introduce a supportive way for the student to continue to listen before responding, such as, "I'm still thinking about what you said and need a few more minutes to think" or "Tell me more about why you think that." Having stems like these in their repertoire affords ELs, as well as students who are timid or who are slower processors, the opportunity to participate actively without feeling pressure to produce before they are ready. Furthermore, when a student uses a stem like this, they are giving the other students the opportunity to think more deeply about how to explain their reasoning so that others can understand. When these students give alternate explanations, they benefit by practicing the content language and having to think flexibly about the concept, while ELs or struggling learners in the group benefit by hearing the concepts expressed in multiple ways. No one is made to feel inadequate or mutely foolish because everyone has both the space and the means to contribute.

Goal-Setting

As we discussed in the previous chapter, all students come to the learning environment with assets that include motivation, aptitudes, social interaction skills, and so on. However, not all their skills are the same; everyone has their own challenges when conversing and collaborating. Being mindful of these challenges, acknowledging them, and setting goals to address them, creates more self-reflection, and consequently, more empathy and self-regulatory behavior. Individual and group goal-setting is an invaluable habit and scaffolding tool to open up safe spaces for successful collaborative conversation.

Hattie (2008) found that goal-setting ranked as one of the top 10 influences that positively impact student achievement because it increases intrinsic motivation and autonomous learning. We have found that in classrooms where students consistently set goals for interaction and share them with the group, they not only become more reflective and self-motivated in their own learning, but become more collaborative, empathetic, and supportive of their peers. By sharing their goals with the group, the students become aware of what each individual is working on and can then help each other to meet their goals.

Goal-setting, as a habit of collaboration, must be practiced intentionally and consistently for it to have an impact. In teachers' classrooms where the Arch system has been established with the most success, the teacher asks the students to use their goal cards before every JPA—the teacher provides time and facilitation for the students to reflect on the goal they had set for themselves the last time they met, and to choose and share the goal they want to set for this session. This accomplishes a couple of things: It makes each student reflect on and take ownership of their own challenges and goals and allows the group to both monitor and aid in their peers' goalkeeping process. Examples of students' goals are: to interrupt less; to make one comment based on a peer's comment; to ask one question; and to not "zone out."

In collaboration with teachers, we have developed individual and group goal card templates that you might find useful in establishing these Habits of Collaboration in your classroom. In Figure 4.1, we have included the four most commonly identified individual challenges and a way to phrase goals addressing them.

When your students reflect on and choose their challenges, remind them that stating it is only the first step. It's not enough to say "My challenge is: I talk too much" and stop there. The pivotal step is selecting a goal and striving to meet it. Therefore, if the challenge is "I talk too much," the goal

Figure 4.1. Individual Goal Card Examples

In conversations,
my challenge is:

 I Interrupt
Others

So my Goal is:

 To allow others
to complete
their thought

In conversations,
my challenge is:

 I Don't Listen
to Others

So my Goal is:

 To listen to others
& build off of
their comments

In conversations,
my challenge is:

 I Don't
Contribute

So my Goal is:

 To make comments
& share my ideas

In conversations,
my challenge is:

 I Talk
Too Much

So my Goal is:

 To encourage
others to talk &
share their ideas

Source: Center for Latino Achievement and Success in Education.

might be "To invite others to share their thoughts." Focusing on the goal, rather than the challenge, allows for self-reflection and intentional practice toward change. That student may always talk more than others, but he or she can be more conscious about how that impacts group dynamics and interactions.

As you guide students through this process, you may want to choose your own goals. Remember that the arc of habits of collaboration run from one side of the Arch to the other, supporting and strengthening both the teacher and the student side. Showing that you are also in the process of goal-setting offers your students a model for their own behavior and lets them know that everyone has challenges. As a note of caution: We often hear teachers say that their challenge is that they talk too much, so their goal is to not talk. They then evaluate themselves based on whether they said anything during the JPA. We encourage the teacher to be a participant, but in the role of facilitator and instructor, questioning and addressing misconceptions. The teacher might want to consider choosing the goal of "encouraging others to speak" or "helping to make sure all voices are heard."

As you are facilitating the goal-setting process, we wish to underscore that it is vital that the students be allowed to choose their own goals. Resist the urge to choose their goals for them *(even if you have a really clear idea of what you think their goal should be)*. This is the only way for the students to truly have agency over the process and to "own" their own learning. Therefore, if a really talkative student decides that her goal is to "share her ideas," allow her to have that goal. Then, when you are debriefing and the students are reflecting on how well they met their goals, you can encourage her by saying, "You have done a great job with this goal; you really shined at expressing your ideas. Maybe now we can try a new goal, like listening to and building off others' ideas?" That way the students still feel they have ownership of the process, will be more self-reflective, and have more buy-in.

Finally, remember that goals can and should change, in part because what is challenging today may not be challenging tomorrow, and in part because what is challenging in one content area might not be challenging in another. For example, we were once talking with a 6th-grade boy who said that his goal in science was to invite others into the conversation because he really liked science and it was a challenge for him to not talk all the time, while in social studies his goal was to share his thoughts more because he didn't feel as confident in that subject. This level of self-reflection is powerful on both a personal and academic level. In Figure 4.2, we have included an example of a rubric used in a lower elementary classroom to help promote self-reflection.

The goals and challenges we have included are only examples and we encourage you to work with your students to create their own goals. This can open up a space for some unique and individualized goals. For example, we were once visiting an 8th-grade ELA class where a group of students was working on a JPA about text structure. All of the students were actively participating, and we noticed that they each had a sticky note before them

Figure 4.2. Individual Goal Reflection Card Example

IC Reflection   So my Goal for next time is:

1 = I did not speak enough during the conversation and/or I was not polite to my friends.

2= I spoke some during the conversation, but I wish I would have shared more and/or I could have been more polite to my friends.

3= I fully partiicpated in the IC. I was polite to my friends when speaking.

with their own handwritten goals. One student in the group lounged back in his chair with an appropriately middle-school surliness about him, and Paula said, "I see you have written your own conversation goals. May I ask what yours is?" The student looked up, his head cocked to one side with a look of indifference, and responded with a sigh, "I have to watch my *tone*." Paula grinned and replied, "I think that's a great goal!" Rather than having someone else reprimand him for responding in a nasty way to his peers, this process allowed for the student to both recognize and take responsibility for his own behavior—thereby creating thoughtful and internalized change.

At the same time that we want to encourage individual goal-setting, we also want to promote reflection on how well the group worked together and helped each other meet their goals. At the end of the JPA, the students look at their goal cards and rate themselves on how well they participated and met their goals. The students then have the opportunity to rate the group's collaboration. That is, the students discuss whether everyone participated substantively and respectfully. In Figure 4.3, we offer two examples of goal-rating cards that teachers have developed to help their students rate how well they have met their individual goals, as well as how well the group has worked together to enact successful conversation and collaboration.

This process of individual and group reflection has profound impacts on how the students behave in other classroom activities as well as outside of the classroom. Teachers and administrators report that children who participate regularly in JPAs tend to be able to mediate conflict with more skill, patience, and equanimity than those who do not. Cafeteria workers, teachers on the playground, and physical education teachers have asked classroom teachers who regularly implement JPAs, "What are you doing in your classroom? These are not the same students I knew."

Consistent anecdotal evidence from teachers and administrators indicate that classrooms fully implementing the Arch system with regularly practiced

Figure 4.3. Group Reflection Card Examples

Group Reflection on Group Work	Individual Reflection on Group Work
What challenges did our group face?	What challenges did I face in our group?
What can we do to address those challenges?	What can I do to address those challenges?
Our goal for next time is:	My goal for next time is:

JPAs, scaffolded by careful planning and mediated by habits of collaboration, create a safe space for students to take linguistic and cognitive risks without fear of ridicule or judgment. Furthermore, these classrooms encourage students to take responsibility for their own learning, practice academic language, and work collaboratively with their peers to solve problems.

THE SCAFFOLDING AND SOCIAL–EMOTIONAL LEARNING (SEL)

The skills and habits of the Arch scaffolding discussed above are grounded in, and help develop, social–emotional skills (e.g., relationship-building, perspective-taking, managing emotions, problem-solving; see CASEL. org for more information). They shift the paradigm for how we interact in classrooms, but because they are embedded in content lessons (such as JPAs), their use has dramatic implications for learning. Therefore, in closing this chapter, we will take a moment to discuss the importance of social–emotional learning (SEL) to academic achievement.

As our students develop social–emotional skills, they will also be developing the skills necessary to interact productively with others—and that interaction is key to cognitive and linguistic development (Lantolf et al., 2015; Swain et al., 2002; Van Lier, 2014). Much work has been done in such fields as neuroscience, psychology, and education linking SEL to academic achievement (Doll, Brehm, & Zucker, 2014; Immordino-Yang & Damasio, 2007; Liew, 2012; Payton, Weissberg, Durlak, Dymnicki, Taylor, Schellinger, & Pachan, 2008); therefore, it becomes critically important that as educators we *intentionally* and *explicitly* make that connection with and for our students.

At the same time, non-cognitive traits, or "soft skills," such as empathy, self-control/awareness, and goal-setting have become the focus of business

---

FOOD FOR THOUGHT

Consider the following quotation and the questions that follow.

"What you learn is that everybody that comes into a room to make decisions is bringing with them the constraints placed upon them . . . and the only way anything gets done is if people recognize the truth of the person across the table. You have to be able to get into their heads and see through their eyes for things to happen."
Barack Obama

Questions to Consider

- What is necessary to "recognize the truth of the person across the table"?
- How is deep listening connected to social–emotional learning?
- How do social–emotional skills like empathy, self–regulation, and goal–setting contribute to successful conversations and productive collaboration?

---

and industry as desired qualities of successful job candidates (McFarlin, 2013). After critical thinking and problem-solving, these aforementioned soft skills, have been identified by managers in a vast array of industries as increasingly important characteristics of successful employees for the role they play in meeting the challenge of finding creative solutions to complex problems (Azim, Gale, Lawlor-Wright, Kirkham, Khan, & Alam, 2010; Deming, 2017; Robles, 2012). Nevertheless, it's stunning how often employers report a lack of candidates who possess these skills, and there is a lot of finger pointing as to who is to blame (Hurrell, 2016). Research shows that in spite of our efforts, students are leaving our schools and entering the workplace woefully ill-equipped to work well with others.

Many K–12 school districts have recently begun to devote a great deal of time to developing their students' SEL; however, the programs implemented and time spent in schools to elevate students' SEL are often seen as something separate from, rather than integral to, academic content learning, even though the 21st-century skills—those skills necessary for students to succeed in the information age (Bellanca & Brandt, 2010)—and state standards call for students to be good collaborators. Teachers frequently try to incorporate SEL within academic content lessons by asking students to work in groups or work with a partner; but these attempts often fall short because students do not have the tools necessary to collaborate, set goals, persist, or communicate clearly in a way that builds on others' thoughts.

Critical thinking and problem-solving skills require levels of student engagement and effort that can only be reached if students have strong social–emotional development.

By employing the scaffolding tools outlined in this chapter, we can help our students to develop and practice these skills as they are learning social studies, math, and science. By embedding these together, we provide our students with the tools needed to more effectively and compassionately interact with increasingly diverse partners. When students are armed with the tools, space, and time to engage in respectful dialogue, to listen to their peers, and to respectfully defend their thoughts without discounting or disparaging the ideas of others, their behaviors often change. Furthermore, their ability to effectively use academic language and manipulate and comprehend complex concepts is dramatically and positively impacted. These life skills are invaluable for all learners, but particularly for culturally and linguistically diverse students.

CHAPTER 5

Integrating the Voussoir Blocks

Enacting Meaningful, Complex, Collaborative, Conversation-Based Lessons

As we discussed in the previous chapters, in the Arch of Collaborative, Conversation-Based Instruction, the columns are formed by the assets that the students and teachers bring to the learning environment and provide the strength to support the Arch structure; however, these assets hold only potential energy and must be "activated" and transformed into kinetic energy through the teacher and student work represented in the *voussoirs* (the wedge-shaped blocks of the semicircular arch). In the language of architecture, the line where the columns and the voussoirs meet is called the *spring line*. In the Arch of collaborative, conversation-based instruction, this name is surprisingly apt because the assets represented in the columns build to that line and then *spring* into action in the arch blocks. The spring line is where the blocks begin to arc toward one another, and it is in the voussoirs that the real work begins.

Recall that the word "voussoir" comes from the Latin root meaning "to turn." Through the activities in these blocks we begin to "turn" and build toward one another, joining the columns of strength into a cohesive structure that will stand alone and support future learning. While this is the most challenging part of the building process, the Arch takes its strength from the turning—it's about both the students *and* teachers turning to meet in the middle. It is here that the teacher's and students' practice and knowledge begin to change through action and interaction. We, as teachers, tend to think that the students should do all the bending—they are the ones in school learning, right? But if we try to utilize only what we know and what we bring to the classroom, without reflecting on what we think or learning from what our students know and bring, then we risk never being able to meet them where they are. If the teacher and students do not *both* bend toward one another and work together to place the blocks well, the structure will fall down. True learning happens when we are co-learners in the process—the magic happens in the middle.

In this chapter, we will look at the final building blocks of the Arch of collaborative, conversation-based instruction. This is where the teachers work on lesson planning, facilitation, and formative assessment, and where the students begin to work together, practicing their skills and deepening their conceptual knowledge, while both teachers and students take full advantage of what all members of the classroom community bring to the learning environment. There are five matching voussoir blocks on each side of the Arch (student side and teacher side). We will go through each of the five voussoir pairs and discuss how they might look in your classroom. As we do, consider how the teacher blocks and the student blocks depend on and support one another, and how the activities they represent work together as a system to form an integrated whole. (To activate your thinking both before and as you read, you may want to complete the JPA Task, Examining the Voussoirs.)

As we begin looking at each of the voussoirs, notice they are laid on top of the spring line that crosses the top of the columns. The first of these is called the *springer*, the block from which all the other blocks "spring." As we "spring into action," let's look at the first fundamental pair of blocks— Language and Literacy—which underscore that all learning, interaction, and collaboration originate in language. In this pair of voussoirs, the teacher must intentionally focus on language and literacy through purposeful planning so that the students can practice language and literacy across the curricula.

LANGUAGE AND LITERACY

The language and literacy voussoirs are perhaps the most familiar of those in the Arch, but for that reason they can be the trickiest. When teaching language and literacy, many teachers find it difficult to find the balance between teaching "form"—focusing on the rules of grammar and vocabulary—and teaching for "function" or meaning—focusing on ensuring that students demonstrate conceptual understanding regardless of how they express it. We may not realize how form and function inform one another and how they are connected: How we say things dramatically impacts how we are understood. Furthermore, we may forget or ignore the importance of all the assets that we bring with us to the classroom regarding language and how those assets can be harnessed for deeper conceptual understanding as well as language development. While our students may not share our home language, social interaction skills, or content literacy skills, it is important

---

JPA TASK CARD: EXAMINING THE VOUSSOIRS

Instructional Goal

To sponsor thinking about how student and teacher activities are similar, how they are different, and how they support one another to activate student and teacher assets and promote learning.

Task Activities

As we move through the voussoirs, with your PLC:

- Think about how the assets in the columns support the voussoirs in the system (refer to the Arch diagram in Figure 1.1).
- Create an H-chart (see Table 5.1) for each of the pairs of voussoir blocks that outlines what that block looks like for the students and teachers.

Questions to Consider

- What do both sides have in common?
- What are the differences?
- What assets directly feed into each voussoir?
- What actions, practices, or activities that you have seen (or can imagine) in your classroom would fit in these blocks?
- How does what the teacher does impact what the students do and vice versa?

---

for us to remember that the skills they bring are invaluable assets that can be activated to help us meet our instructional goals.

Form or Function?

The tension between function and form, what something does and how it does it, represents a central problem in language teaching, or teaching in general. In language, *form* relates to how we say things—our use of words and the way we structure our sentences, etc.— while the *function* refers to the content of what we are saying—the ideas, thoughts, questions, emotions, etc. that what we say evokes. Historically, in education, the urgent pressure to transmit prescribed standards has led teachers to focus on *how* students are saying things, the form, and to lose sight of *what* they are saying or if they are making meaning. This becomes particularly salient if they are using language and expressing thoughts in new and unusual ways. Therefore, we as teachers ought to question our focus. Do we focus on form? Or do we focus on function?

Table 5.1. Sample H-Chart

Students Only	Both	Teacher Only
Working on Language and Literacy Development		Focusing on Students' Language and Literacy Development
Making Meaningful Connections		Contextualizing Lessons for Meaning
Engaging in Challenging and Complex Activities		Designing Challenging and Complex Activities
Working in Collaboration with Others		Creating Opportunities for Collaboration
Learning through Purposeful Conversation		Teaching through Purposeful Conversation

This question is central to language teaching. Lightbown and Spada (2013) discuss the disputes among second language education researchers about the best way to teach language and find that there is a real tension between focus on *form* (e.g., grammar, structure, vocabulary) and focus on *function* (i.e., language in use). Educators' theoretical frameworks and end goals determine their focus. In traditional classrooms, it is often believed that "teaching language" implies focusing explicitly and exclusively on language forms or grammar without embedding that instruction in activities that show how language is actually used or practiced. In traditional language arts lessons, teachers often focus on conjugating verbs, diagramming sentences, and categorizing sentence types to the exclusion of meaning-based content and without offering students authentic opportunities to think about and practice using language. However, although we often measure proficiency by a student's knowledge of grammar, knowing how to conjugate verbs correctly is not a guarantee that a student will be able to speak or write with competence and proficiency. Similarly, fluency in a language doesn't mean a student can identify the tenses and word categories or write with grammar-book correctness. I'm sure we all know many native speakers of English who could never identify what a past participle is but can use one in a sentence perfectly.

Constructivist or sociocultural models of instruction are based on the idea that language is learned through interaction, and meaning is created through mediated tools (such as language). This means that collaboration and conversation are essential to cognitive development and language learning. Researchers who study the role of interaction on language development suggest that we provide students with varied and authentic opportunities to

FOOD FOR THOUGHT: WHERE DO WE FOCUS? FORM OR FUNCTION?

Consider the following passage and the questions that follow.

Recently Paula had the opportunity to see the *Joris Laarman Lab: Design in the Digital Age* exhibition at the High Museum in Atlanta. Laarman and his team use cutting-edge technology to create ultra-modern furniture that explores the tension between practical use and the importance of aesthetics and ornament. His designs, which bring together ideas from an interdisciplinary team of scientists, artists, and craftspeople, include deep-seated rocking chairs that emulate the structure of bones, digitally printed Rococo tables, and one particularly beautiful (yet practical) piece: a radiator designed as a curlicued wall sculpture whose curves are not only aesthetically pleasing, but make it more effective in serving its purpose of heating the surrounding space by increasing the radiator's surface area.

One looks at some of Laarman's designs and wonders at the fact that while they may not follow traditional forms—his chairs don't look like "normal" chairs and that radiator didn't look like any Paula had ever seen before—they make sense for the purpose that they were theoretically designed. Their forms meet their functions, but they do so in unique and heretofore unseen ways. So, in order to appreciate these designs, one must stop thinking for the moment about what a radiator is supposed to look like and think instead about what its purpose is and then ask, "Does it do what it must? Does the form detract from its ability to do its job?" Only then can one appreciate both the beauty of the piece as well as its functionality.

Questions to Consider

- How are form and function connected in teaching language and content?
- How do we balance teaching form (i.e., Standard American English) and content (social studies, science, math, ELA Standards) so that students can make meaning by using their language resources to understand complex concepts?
- How can our students use their entire repertoire of linguistic assets to create new but understandable language forms that meet the conceptual functions we would like them to achieve?

interact and discuss problems, relating instructional activities to what the students already know (Lantolf et al., 2015) and pushing them to practice and explore new boundaries of knowledge without expressly focusing on grammatical forms (Watanabe & Swain, 2007).

Which theory (and consequently which method) educators choose depends greatly on what our end goals are, but focusing on form and focusing on function need not be mutually exclusive. Teaching language form (that is, decontextualized vocabulary or verb conjugations) without embedding them in meaningful context may give students a lot of words but not a lot of understanding or ability to actually do anything with them. There is another option (one that the collaborative conversation system supports): that, in spite of what might appear to be clashing theoretical frames, we do some combination of both—focusing on form (that is, grammar and structure of language) while being mindful of function—making meaning of complex content material through collaborative interaction. If we want our students to interact productively, using language to collaborate and solve problems, then we must provide them with ample opportunities to use and practice *real* language. The goal of such activities is to produce meaning-filled communication, while striving to help students become proficient users of standard academic English with an awareness and command of the rules and functions of each of the languages in their repertoires and a knowledge of when and how to use them to meet their specific goals. In the end, whether we focus on form (how they speak), or function (what they say and what it means), or both, in our instruction, one thing is clear: We must keep our students central to our focus.

The Role of Error Correction and Corrective Feedback. The challenge for the teacher is to find the form/function balance and decide what corrective feedback and instruction to provide and when to provide it. This requires knowing your students—paying careful attention to what they say and how they say it, while understanding that errors or silence may not be indicators that the student is not learning. A quiet student can be thinking and building linguistic and conceptual knowledge. A student can use a grammatical structure correctly one day, get it wrong the next, and actually be advancing in language development. Furthermore, speakers make sense with all kinds of forms that are not proper according to the grammar books. So when and how should we correct our students' language use, especially when we want them to collaborate and feel safe practicing language?

Research regarding corrective feedback offers some answers. While it is not good to correct every "error" when it happens (this impedes communication and will often be so demoralizing that the student will shut down), targeted correction is better than ignoring errors and is moderated by the degree of explicitness (Hartshorn, Evans, Merrill, Sudweeks, Strong-Krause, & Anderson, 2010; Sheen, 2010). The Corrective Feedback Chart (Table 5.2) shows a set of corrective feedback strategies ordered from least to most explicit. Think about these strategies as you read the Food for Thought titled "Error or Evidence of Multiple Linguistic Repertoires?" and consider how we can help students make meaning as they learn new language forms.

Table 5.2. Corrective Feedback Chart

Modeling	Teacher (or peer) uses academic language or standard form to model for the student.
Clarification Requests	"I'm sorry, what did you say?"
Paralingual Signals	Teacher uses facial expressions or other nonverbal cues to call student attention to an error (e.g., wrinkling brow, cocking head).
Repetition	Teacher repeats the word or phrase stressing the "error," often using rising intonation to call the student's attention to the error (e.g., student says "I go yesterday" and the teacher repeats, "I GO yesterday?" stressing the error in tense).
Recasts	Student says: "We go yesterday to the store." Teacher responds: "Oh, you went to the store yesterday?"
Elicitations	"We call the place where the river meets the sea the . . . ?"
Explicit Correction	"In Standard American English we say XYZ."
Metalinguistic Commentary	The teacher explains the rule or draws explicit attention to the difference between the standard form and the form in another language or variety.

The Role of Translanguaging

Translanguaging describes the process of using all the linguistic (and non-linguistic) resources at one's disposal—often crossing the boundaries of languages and combining them in novel ways to make sense (e.g., writing *uata* rather than *water*—spelling the English word as you would if you were writing in Spanish). It is sometimes difficult for us to recognize when our students are using the breadth of their linguistic assets to be understood (particularly if we don't speak the languages or language varieties that our students speak or if we have strong biases against those languages or language varieties). However, our students often translanguage, using what they know in one language and applying it consciously or unconsciously to other languages. When the people that the students are talking to don't have access to all the linguistic resources that the students have, it can be difficult for them to interpret or understand what the students mean, and what they say can sound like an "error." So, for example, our students may try to make meaning by looking for cognates (and we should encourage them to do so), but when they land upon a false cognate (as when a Spanish speaker says that they will "assist" a meeting but what they meant to say was that they

FOOD FOR THOUGHT: ERROR OR EVIDENCE OF MULTIPLE LINGUISTIC REPERTOIRES?

Consider the following passage and the questions that follow.

Our team was recently analyzing a set of writing samples from a group of 4th-grade English language learners whose home language was Spanish, to see if Instructional Conversations had an impact on their individual writing performance. The samples were collected from among a larger set of county-wide constructed-response writing assessments designed to prepare the students for the state-mandated annual end-of-year standardized tests. For the assessment, the students were asked to respond to a narrative prompt about a dog named Spike and to complete the story. Because some students had used non-standard grammatical forms as well as non-standard spelling, at times the coders had trouble reading the responses and understanding what the students wanted to say—this made it difficult to assess their conceptual understanding and linguistic competence.

In one of our weekly meetings, we were discussing the coding process, reading through particularly complicated passages, and deciding how to interpret them. One student had written: "Iso jot we give Spike uata." None of us had figured out what she meant until, reading the phrase out loud, something clicked: It made sense. The student had meant to write, "It was so *hot*, we gave Spike *water*." She had written "jot" and "uata" because she knew how the words sounded in English and although she didn't know how to spell them, she used the resources she had to spell them phonetically *in Spanish*. She was connecting her oral language in English to what she knew about writing systems—transferring what she knew about writing in Spanish into her English writing. She had made some brilliant cross-linguistic transfers, but because we were blinded by our own focus on Standard English spelling, we were unable, until we read the phrase out loud, to recognize what she had done. We were able to see that the "w" in English words is pronounced "oo" like the Spanish vowel "u." So while this student had technically made an error in Standard English spelling, she had used all her linguistic assets to make meaning. Had we not stopped to consider what those assets were, we would not have been able to recognize her action and would have not been able to accurately assess her abilities or understanding. Nor would we have been able to use this assessment as a tool for strategically targeting our future instruction to help her take the next step toward mastery of Standard English.

Questions to Consider

- What strategies can we as teachers employ to recognize and assess when our students are using their assets?
- How can we support students in activating and intentionally transferring what they know from their multiple repertoires to master Standard English?

will "attend," because the word *asistir* in Spanish means "to attend"), we may not see that they are using their assets and see only that they didn't use the English word as an English speaker might be accustomed to. This isn't an "error"; it's a breakdown in the process of meaning-making because our assets and their assets are too far apart. When our students translanguage, they are doing creative, complicated linguistic work. But meaning-making is a collaborative process that requires that all participants work together to build understanding. To bridge the distance created by different lived experiences and linguistic repertoires, we can do two things: build students' metalinguistic awareness so they can be intentional about their language use, and reflect about our own repertoires while learning more about theirs. This way we can both make ourselves better understood and identify and accurately interpret what they are saying. By supporting students' translanguaging, you can: capitalize on their linguistic assets, strengthen their metalinguistic awareness, support their Standard English literacy, and build their self-confidence.

Building Metalinguistic Awareness. Teachers can facilitate students' metalinguistic awareness—an understanding of how language works in both form and function—and help them access their home language as an asset by designing lessons that, in addition to teaching a content concept, also engage them in reflecting on how language is structured and used to make meaning. As you listen to your students interact in collaborative conversations, you can help build metalinguistic awareness (Bialystok & Barac, 2012) and offer them targeted corrective feedback (El Tatawy, 2002; Ellis, 2008) (see Table 5.2) to guide them to notice the linguistic forms they are using, how their home language is structured compared to Standard American English, and what strategies they can employ to use all their language repertoires with more agency and intention.

In addition to valuing our students' home language(s), this process gives students a sense of efficacy and control over their own learning and engenders self-regulation and independence. When students have a clear sense of how language works, they gain a greater capacity to see how to apply what they know about language to unfamiliar situations.

Ofelia Garcia and her colleagues at the CUNY-New York State Initiative for Emergent Bilinguals have developed strategies for supporting students' abilities to access and activate all of their linguistic assets in the classroom (Celic & Seltzer, 2011; García & Kleyn, 2016). Here are a few ideas for how you can begin to help your students activate and harness their linguistic assets to develop their language proficiency and deepen their conceptual understanding:

JPA Task Card: Creating Lessons that Harness Student Translanguaging

Instructional Goal

To reflect on the building blocks of *Language and Literacy* and how to activate student language assets and the role they can play in instruction.

Task Activities

With your PLC:

- Consider the JPA Student Task Card: Exploring the Water Cycle.
- Adapt this task for another topic or academic subject.

Questions to Consider

- How would an activity like this utilize your students' translanguaging to aid in their intentional activation of their linguistic assets?
- How might a task like this be modified for students whose home language is not Spanish?
- How might this support language development of native English speakers or speakers of non-standard varieties of English?
- How could building an understanding of how languages are structured facilitate the cognitive and linguistic development of all students?

Student JPA Task Card: Exploring the Water Cycle

Instructional Goal

To explore the water cycle by connecting prior knowledge in content and language to new information.

Task Activities

In your group:

- Examine the chart with words and images from the Water Cycle.
- Fill in the missing words.
- Draw a diagram using the words and pictures to illustrate the water cycle.

Question to Consider

- What do you notice about the words in English compared to Spanish?

English Word	Spanish Word	Visual Representation
Aquifer		
Prescipitation	Precipitación	
Evaporation	Evaporación	
Condensation		
Cycle	Ciclo	

- *Create multilingual word walls and label objects in the classroom in multiple languages.* This will familiarize students with the written forms of words they are learning or already know and strengthen literacy in the languages of the students in your classroom.
- *Utilize cognate charts.* Encourage metalinguistic awareness by helping your students examine what they already know about language and literacy in their home language and actively transfer that to English language learning.
- *Provide access to books and media resources in the languages of your students.* Having bilingual or translated materials, multilingual listening centers, bilingual and picture dictionaries in your classroom, and using such strategies as comparing texts on the same subject in multiple languages helps students build biliteracy while utilizing home language assets. This can also increase family engagement.
- *Offer all students the chance to speak and share what they know.* Even newcomers can begin to collaborate in conversations about content if given the right tools.
  - » Provide sentence stems, word banks, and semi-preconstructed phrases to scaffold for students who do not yet have sufficient language abilities in English.
  - » Co-construct narratives with interactive writing exercises.
  - » Create opportunities for students to discuss terms or concepts that you are teaching with each other in their home languages as well as in English, thereby strengthening their connections and understanding and offering all students a chance to learn something new.
  - » Do not restrict meaning-making to spoken and written language. Provide opportunities to use multi-modal literacies (realia, graphics, manipulatives, gestures, artwork, movement, music, etc.). This values what students know rather than signaling—or shaming them for—what they don't know.
- *Group students intentionally to take advantage of and support all students' linguistic assets.* Depending on your instructional goal, you may want to group students of varying language ability together. Students can model language for one another while supporting their conceptual understanding. At the same time, do not be afraid to put students with the same home language in collaborative groups together. This allows them to receive a fuller and deeper understanding of the concepts while learning the language. Additionally, although the students may not need to use their home language for support, simply having a peer who shares the same cultural and

linguistic background can often reduce the stress of performing within the group.

- **Create spaces for co-learning by asking your students about key words and phrases in your students' home language(s).** This strategy helps build a safe learning environment where your students can see themselves as experts and you as a learner. Additionally, this strategy can provide you with tools for scaffolding because as you begin to build knowledge about how English differs from your students' languages, you can help spark their curiosity and their understanding of how to leverage that knowledge to their advantage.

Metalinguistic Awareness of Disciplinary Languages. As teachers in CLD classrooms, we are charged with facilitating students' development of both Standard American English and academic language. So in planning our lessons to support our students in their apprenticeship as users of academic language, let us not forget that there is not one single "academic English" but rather a range of Englishes specific to different disciplines. That is to say, disciplines differ in the kinds of language, topics, genres and structures used; learning to think and communicate in one discipline is different from learning to think and communicate in another discipline (Christie & Maton, 2011). Therefore, we encourage teachers to consider distinct disciplinary languages and models to practice as they plan collaborative, conversation-based lessons, and to capitalize on their own expertise in their field to choose goals for language and literacy development that will support their content instructional goals. As you teach science or social studies or math, you must also be mindful of teaching the language of each and the ways that arguments are made and information is presented in those disciplines. This requires teachers to be thoughtful about how language is used in each of these disciplines and be more explicit about teaching it, beyond giving students vocabulary lists to memorize. The more explicit teachers are about the language of different disciplinary genres and the more opportunities students have to practice them, the more agency students will develop in their learning of both language and content.

Language and Identity

One last thought as we contemplate language and literacy and how we may activate our students' language assets for instructional purposes—while we may consider that one of our instructional goals is to guide our students to a mastery of Standard American English, we must not forget, as Nelson

---

FOOD FOR THOUGHT

Read the quotation and consider the questions that follow.

> "In order to succeed, I had to stop talking like the people I came from and who I loved, and start talking like those that never thought I'd amount to anything."
> Anonymous Teacher

Questions to Consider

- How can we support our students' use of all their linguistic repertoires and the identities that they represent while guiding them toward a mastery of Standard English?
- How might our students feel if they believe that they must "choose" between their home and school languages/selves?
- What impacts might it have for our students if we do not recognize and embrace all the language(s) they bring with them as part of their identity?

Flores says, that translanguaging, and by extension language learning, are "political acts" (Flores, 2014) which have implications for students' identities within and beyond the classroom walls. Language learners' lives are integral to their learning process. Their desire to learn a language is often guided more by their perception of how that language can contribute to their individual agency and personal identity than it is by the value they see in the language itself (McKay & Wong, 1996). As a consequence, if learners wish to take on the identity that a new language represents for them they will invest in it, but only as long as this identity has cultural capital within their social sphere (Darvin & Norton, 2015).

Learning a second language (or variety of language) can pose a challenge to one's identity because it can stretch the boundaries of who we perceive ourselves to be and how others perceive us (Cummins et al., 2005; Ibrahim, 1999). Additionally, what constitutes cultural capital for one individual might not function this way for another, depending on their goals of social acceptance and interaction. Consider how a person who speaks a nonstandard variety of English might be received by their community if they begin to speak Standard American English at home. They may be seen as inauthentic, accused of trying to be something they are not.

Therefore, as we reflect on our own assets and our own biases, we may find it startling to discover that becoming a speaker of Standard American

---

NOTES FROM THE FIELD

Consider the following passage and the questions that follow.

Last spring, Paula visited a preschool that was trying to introduce Spanish to the English-speaking students by sharing words and phrases every day to help them develop some bilingual awareness. The school asked Paula if she wouldn't mind reading a story in Spanish to the students in one of the pre-K rooms. Paula was delighted at the opportunity to participate in this activity and immediately went to the library to check out a picture book with a story that would be familiar to them. She hoped to activate the students' background knowledge and give them context, while introducing the "new" language in a way that would capitalize on their linguistic knowledge and allow them to make connections.

As she read the story to the class, Paula used gestures, inflections, and questions in Spanish while pointing to the illustrations that matched the words she was using. The children interacted enthusiastically with Paula as she read the story, but afterwards, one child confided to Paula that initially she didn't recognize that the story was *The Three Little Pigs*. She had been completely lost at first, despite Paula's playacting and the benefit of the pictures, until the part where the Wolf: *"Se bufó y se sopló y derribó la casa!"* or *"He huffed and he puffed and he blew the house down!"* At that moment, the child had something to hang her prior knowledge on and was able to follow the story. From there on, she began to catch and retain words and was able to accurately respond in English to questions posed in Spanish about what would happen next using the patterns she had learned.

Being able to attach the Spanish narrative to what she knew about the story in English was the key to her unlocking that previously closed door to language and understanding. Once she had found the hook, the rest of the story made absolute sense to her. She then knew what was going on and was able to connect it to what she already knew, thereby beginning to learn words and phrases in the new language.

Questions to Consider

- How does making connections to what we already know facilitate learning?
- What strategies can teachers use to activate and connect background knowledge?
- How does responding in our first language show that we are processing words and concepts in our "new" language?

English may not be a goal to which all of our students aspire. They may resist learning and using Standard American English for reasons of identity and group membership. These are issues that we as teachers must address and make explicit in our efforts to give our students more agency with their language(s) and their learning, so that they might embrace and value all their language assets and the selves they represent.

CONTEXTUALIZATION

The second pair of voussoir blocks in the Arch of collaborative, conversation-based instruction represents contextualization. These blocks are placed directly on top of the voussoir blocks representing language and literacy; contextualization is often built on the meaning that students construct through the use of language. To contextualize lessons and help students make meaningful connections to academic language and concepts, teachers must capitalize on the language(s) and activate the background knowledge that students bring with them. These connections lead to deeper content understanding and make their school-based learning real and relevant. Putting lessons in context helps students connect their school lives with the rest of their lives and answer the question, "Why do I care?"; engages them, so that all students feel like they are welcome and included; leads students to deeper understanding of academic content; and offers a means for teachers to differentiate content to meet all their students' needs (especially those of CLD students).

The Role of Prior Knowledge and Applying what We Already Know

The purpose of providing contextual clues and activating background knowledge—what our students already know—is to help them intentionally (and with metacognitive awareness) attach what they know to what we want them to know (Perin, 2011). When students arrive at school they don't "come with nothing." They have lives outside school, and what they do and experience in their homes, their communities, their places of worship, and elsewhere become part of their internal geographies—shaping who they are and what they know. Their lived experiences provide them with knowledge about all kinds of things, including their values, humor, work, religious practices, and of course language. These funds of knowledge that are influenced by numerous and cross-cutting factors such as culture, social class, age, family, and so on impact what they know and how they can connect

NOTES FROM THE FIELD: CONNECTING BACKGROUND KNOWLEDGE TO SCHOOL-BASED LEARNING

Last summer, as part of an international teacher exchange project, our team had the privilege of visiting an organic coffee farm in Costa Rica with a group of technical high school teachers from Georgia. Three of the teachers with us taught agriculture and were fascinated by the similarities and differences between their farming experience in the Appalachian foothills of Georgia and what they saw on this small parcel of land nestled on the side of a mountain in a tropical cloud forest of Central America. As we walked through the coffee plantation, one of the teachers asked Roberto, the farmer, why the rows of coffee plants didn't have the neat, raked look that one might expect in a planted field. The densely-leaved, squat bushes had copious leaf litter piled around their bases, and had banana plants and citrus trees growing in and around them in a seemingly random pattern. Nevertheless, the plants looked healthy. Their flexible branches were covered in glossy, dark green leaves interspersed with tightly-grouped bunches of deep-red coffee cherries.

Roberto smiled at the question and replied that it was all part of the organic farming process. He apologized for how messy the field looked, but then he explained why. He was eloquent in his description of how he pruned the plants, leaving the cuttings around the roots where they could serve multiple purposes: preventing erosion, maintaining moisture in the soil, and providing nutrients to the plants as they decomposed. The banana plants and citrus trees were not random in their placement but served as companion plants providing shade for the coffee and attracting pollinators while dissuading insects and birds from predating the coffee. He explained that organic farming, particularly in the tropics where fungus and insects were rampant, was slow and labor intensive and didn't produce as big a crop as non-organic methods, but paid off in the end because it was more sustainable, avoided the need for chemical fertilizers and pesticides, and promoted more robust biodiversity.

The Georgia farmers had never considered how shifting to organic farming might impact not only chemical use, but how a field might look. They wanted to know more. Roberto continued, discussing the rigorous and intensive organic certification process (it took 6 years, several training courses, piles of documentation, and four farm inspections a year). As he described the daunting nature of the process, we were all struck by a comment that he made. He said, "I was really worried about the certification courses because I don't have a college degree and they [the teachers] were scientists. But I realized in the middle of the first course that all the concepts they were teaching were things that I had learned from the time I was a child, working at my grandfather's side. I just never had the name for them."

**NOTES FROM THE FIELD: CONNECTING BACKGROUND KNOWLEDGE
TO SCHOOL-BASED LEARNING, CONTINUED**

Roberto had vast embodied knowledge from his lived experience that he was able to access and apply to the complicated and challenging task of organic farming, but in order to obtain certification, he had to learn the academic and technical language necessary to document and communicate to his teachers what he knew.

Questions to Consider

- How did the Georgian Ag teachers' background knowledge impact how they saw and interpreted the coffee field?
- How might hearing Roberto's story help them to connect to and reflect on what they already knew?
- How do you think Roberto's recognition that he had a lifetime of experiences to draw on helped him successfully gain organic farming certification?
- What kinds of embodied knowledge from their lived experiences do our students bring with them?
- How can we find out what embodied knowledge our students bring and help them access it to meet our instructional goals?

---

to the academic concepts that we want them to learn (González, Moll, & Amanti, 2006; Moll et al., 1992).

However, applying the background knowledge our students have learned through experience to the classroom can be complicated, in part, because that experiential learning is often tacit or what is referred to in cognitive and neuroscience as *embodied* knowledge—knowledge that lies under the surface of consciousness and is not easily accessible to the conscious mind (Adloff, Gerund, & Kaldewey, 2015). Our students often know a great deal about what we are trying to teach them, but do not know how to activate their embodied knowledge and to connect it to class. For example, students whose families work in farming may know a great deal about horticulture and plant science, but they may not know how to access and apply that knowledge in the classroom. They may think that because they didn't learn what they know from a book, and don't yet know the academic language for what they know, that their knowledge is somehow not legitimate. Students often don't know what they already know or how to connect it to what they are learning in school, unless we talk about it. Until then, it can be difficult for students to make sense of new knowledge, even when it is directly connected to their prior knowledge. This was the case for the pre-K student in the previous Note from the Field. Although the student was very familiar with the story of the three little pigs, she was lost during the reading until she became conscious of the connection to what she already knew (*"Se bufó y se sopló y derribó la casa!"* was the same as *"He huffed and he puffed and he blew the house down!"* in Spanish). The phrase repeated by the wolf provided a cord she could use to consciously attach what she knew from the story in English to the story in Spanish and give the words meaning. The more students are able to access what they know from their lived experience and connect it to new experiences, the more coherent, confident, and engaged they will be in their learning. Our role as teachers lies in planning our lessons so that our students can make those kinds of connections.

However, identifying and activating students' background knowledge can be challenging because although, as the Arch describes, we all come with funds of knowledge, teachers' funds of knowledge may differ sharply from those of their students. And people are not always aware that what's normal for them is not normal for everyone. They can suffer from a kind of ethnocentrism of the majority, and begin to believe that the way they do things, think, or believe is not just *a* way of doing things, but the *right* way. This can lead teachers to believe that if students don't know the things that they know or do things the way they do, that their students are not normal, or have deficits that need fixing. So as we teachers begin to think about contextualizing academic content for our students, we must be self-reflective about what we know. We must avoid some overarching assumptions, such as:

- everyone thinks like we think;
- if our students don't look, talk, speak, or act like us, we can't contextualize for them;
- or conversely, if our students do look, talk, speak, or act like us, their experience must be the same as ours.

In order to contextualize for students, teachers have to learn about who they are, where they are from, and what and how they think. In the section that follows we will be discussing in detail ways to become self-reflective and to listen to our students in order to better contextualize academic content for them.

Linguistic Relativity and What it Means for Teaching

While contextualizing lessons for students to help them intentionally access their background knowledge and apply and transfer their home language skills to the school environment, it is important to keep in mind that language and culture impact cognition. In the early 20th century, linguistic anthropologists Edward Sapir and his student Benjamin Whorf developed what is now known as the Sapir-Whorf Hypothesis (or linguistic relativism) (Thomson, 2006). This refers to the concept that language influences thoughts, behavior, and how people construct reality. In basic terms, the hypothesis suggests that the language we speak shapes how we see the world, and the way we see the world shapes how we talk and interact with those around us. The kaleidoscope flux of impressions and information received through the senses is constantly being filtered for importance, sorted, or discarded largely through linguistic systems. We cut this information up, organize it into concepts, and ascribe significances to it as we do. These concepts, and the meanings we give to them, are constructed through interactions with other people and are codified in the patterns of our language. But not all languages categorize concepts in the same way (some even have the same meanings attached to different phenomena); this impacts our neural networks—the system of interconnected neurons that we use to process and transfer information (Xia, Xu, & Mo, 2018). That is to say, the way we talk and what we talk about actually changes the physical structure of our brains.

An interesting example of this is when an English-speaker looks at a rainbow, he or she generally perceives at least six separate color bands, because that is largely how we categorize colors in English—we have names for red, orange, yellow, green, blue, and purple. By contrast, speakers of Shona, a language spoken in Zimbabwe, may only "see" three color bands. They lump together orange, red, and purple into one category, blue and green into another, and yellow and light green into a third, because their language has words for these color boundaries. This demonstrates that we are not led by the same physical evidence to the same picture of the universe; unless our linguistic and cultural backgrounds are similar, and even when those are shared, context matters tremendously.

This is important for teachers because this means that learning a new language, and the concepts associated with it, is not just a matter of "translation" (what we often think of as a simple matter of replacing one word for another). It is often about learning a new way to view the world—the

way we categorize knowledge and the language associated with it is very culturally bound. Take a look at the two pictures on this page. What are they? You probably said, "That's easy! Those are owls!" You might have said that the one on the right is a horned owl (or hoot owl), and the one on the left a barn owl (or screech owl)—but still, they're both owls. However, for many Spanish speakers (at least those from Costa Rica and other parts of Central America), the one on the left is a *buho,* and the one on the right is a *lechuza.* These are not just two different kinds of owls, but two different kinds of birds, as different as ducks and geese.

Now look at the two pictures on the next page. What are they?

The one on the left is a butterfly, right? And the one on the right is a moth? English speakers tend to think these two insects belong to totally different categories, but most Spanish speakers do not. The insect on the left is a *mariposa*, but so is the one on the right. It's just that one is a *mariposa diurna* and the other is a *mariposa nocturna*: you guessed it—a daytime butterfly and a nighttime butterfly. So as a teacher, if you hear your students refer to a moth as a butterfly, you might assume that they don't know what a moth is, when in fact they are simply transferring what they know from Spanish and applying it to English.

So if language helps to shape how people compartmentalize the world, determining how we see and conceptualize things, what happens when our language has concepts that don't exist in another language, or vice versa? What happens when the categories overlap or conflict? And what does this mean for us as teachers?

Levels of Contextualization

Contextualizing lessons is perhaps the hardest of the voussoir blocks to plan for and execute, because it is hard for people to reflect on what they think of as normal, or to get out of their own contextual boxes, see things from another's perspective, and incorporate that perspective into teaching. In working with teachers, we found that they understood *why* contextualizing lessons was important, but *how* to do it was harder to see. In response, we have developed a four-level pyramid (Figure 5.1) to help teachers think about how to contextualize lessons. Levels I and II build the safe environment and start with the teacher's point of view, or lens, to begin to make connections, from that perspective, to students' experiences. At levels III and IV the teacher begins to draw out and listen to students' perspectives, to reconsider their own, and to modify instruction to incorporate their students' experiences and understandings. As you read through levels I through IV, notice that the perspective shifts from being exclusively from the teacher's point of view to an opening to and recognition of students' contributions, experiences, and understandings, to finally being more reciprocal and reflective, where both the teacher's and the students' understanding change as a result of interacting with each other and the content. Each level has indicators to help teachers envision how to make lessons real and relevant for students, thereby helping them to make connections to what they already know, as well as examples and points of danger to be cautious of. As you move through the levels, remember that each level is important, and wherever you are, you should give yourself a pat on the back. The purpose of this analysis is to give teachers a place to identify with and ideas of where to shift their thinking and practice, so that they can more intentionally listen to—and contextualize content for—their students.

Figure 5.1. Levels of Contextualization

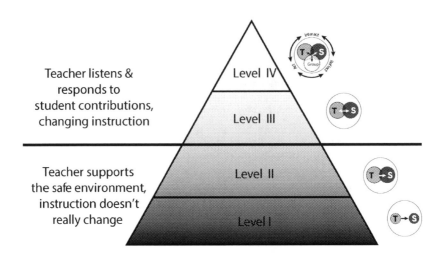

Level I: The Teacher Lens. At level I, the teacher uses what she or he knows to contextualize content for the class. This is the appropriate level for the beginning of the year when you don't yet know your students and must rely on your own resources and knowledge base. At this level, the teacher *notices* and *recognizes* students' contexts and individual differences. It is essential to start by acknowledging that students are not all the same, and that they come with unique lived experiences that we teachers must learn about and tap into in order to help them achieve academically and engage socially.

One of the most important things a teacher can do at this level to establish trust and a safe learning environment is to learn and use students' names, trying to pronounce them as the students wish to have them said. That means that teachers don't decide what the student should be called—even with the best of intentions. Ask the students what they want to be called, and if the class roll says the student's name is Jorge, and he wishes to be called Jorge, then that is what he should be called. But but he says that he wishes to be called George, then that is what you should call him. The student may have good reasons for wanting to be called George: to avoid pressure from peers, to assimilate, or to please teachers or parents (or some other reason entirely). You may privately ask him why he wishes to be called George rather than Jorge, but you must allow him to choose his name. Names mark identities, and teachers need to honor the identities students choose.

At this level, the teacher also uses "common knowledge" to contextualize for the student, calling on references that are familiar and that the students

---

JPA TASK CARD: LEVELS OF CONTEXTUALIZATION

Instructional Goal

To reflect on the voussoir blocks of the Arch representing *Contextualizing Lessons for Meaning/Making Meaningful Connections,* how to activate them, and the role they might play in instruction.

Task Activities

- On paper or a whiteboard create a four-square chart, labeling the squares:

  Level I   Level II   Level III   Level IV

- Consider the images in Figure 5.1 and what they show us about the relationship between the students and the teachers in the classroom
- Consider who is doing the talking, how the class is arranged, and other factors that might impact how much the teacher can learn about the students from the interaction portrayed.
- Write your ideas and place them in the corresponding quadrants as you progress.

Questions to Consider

- What does a teacher need to do to actively contextualize for students?
- How might each level help to enact and deepen understanding?
- When have you reached each level in your classroom?

---

will likely know and connect to. Among these are references to popular culture, sporting events, and places and events in the neighborhood or school. The teacher can also take advantage of the information that teachers have access to, such as students' school records (or information about the students' families or background, etc.) to connect to the students and to help make them feel that each one of them is an important member of the class.

Level I Example: The teacher uses students' names, mentions places they're from, and invites families to share cultural information.

Level I Dangers:
- Students are not involved in the process of identifying contextual clues.
- Curriculum is not added to or changed.
- What you think you know can be deceiving—what is "common knowledge" for you may not be for your students.

Level II: Teacher Lens of Shared Experience. Like Level I, the main purpose of Level II is to create a safe and welcoming environment where our students feel part of the class. While Level II is still from the teacher's perspective, at this level, the teacher deliberately *finds* and *creates* shared knowledge to contextualize lessons for the students. That might mean investigating students' interests or backgrounds in order to include references to them in lessons. This can also mean creating school-based background knowledge and shared experiences to refer to when teaching. At this level, the teacher begins to integrate knowledge about students' home/school/world to plan and provide intentional opportunities for students to make meaningful connections.

Level II Example: You know that many of your students come from the Mexican state of Michoacán, and you also know that the monarch butterflies migrate to Michoacán every year. Therefore, you look up information about Mexico and the monarchs, and you talk about that when you do your 2nd-grade butterfly life cycle unit as a way to help your students feel connected to the lesson.

Level II Dangers:
- Students don't contribute.
- Common ground is still on the teacher's terms.
- What teachers learn (or assume) about students may not help them make meaningful connections—for example, though students' families come from Michoacán and the butterflies do indeed migrate there, the students may never have seen the migration. (Think about how many students who live in cities near a coast but have never been to the beach.)

Level III: Teacher Facilitated with Student Lens. Level III is where the teacher begins to invite the students to contribute more to his or her understanding of them as people and thinkers. The teacher intentionally creates opportunities to learn about students and how they see the world. The safe environment developed in Levels I and II is vital here as it provides a foundation of a safe space for students to share their ideas and not feel at risk. Also critical to this level is the teacher's willingness and commitment to listen openly to students as they express their ideas and discuss their views and lived experiences. This listening can happen in the lunchroom, in the hallway, or when students make connections during lessons. This may mean allowing students to talk for a moment about these connections, even if they seem unrelated to the instructional goal. What may look like unrelated rabbit holes may be pivotal in shifting thinking about how to connect instruction to students' background knowledge. Shared connections can help teachers formatively assess, differentiate, and plan for better contextualization, so that the curriculum is real and relevant for the students. At this point, the teacher deliberately and mindfully integrates what he or she has learned into lesson plans, so that the students may connect their learning to what they know and see ways that lessons apply to them and their lives.

Level III Example: You have learned through listening to your students' interactions that one student, Xiaoli, is a fanatic for Ferraris, while another, Gerardo, is a big Georgia Bulldog fan. In a JPA whose instructional goal is to ensure that the students can identify types of sentences (e.g., fragment, simple, complex, compound), you create a sorting activity with sentences that incorporate the students' names and their interests. For example, "Xiaoli's Ferrari was making knocking noises, so she took it to the mechanic." Or, "Gerardo went to Sanford Stadium on Saturday to see the big Georgia–Auburn game." By including the students' names and interests in the lesson, you increase both engagement and motivation—even for what could be a dry grammar lesson—while creating meaningful connections that the students will remember more readily.

Level III Dangers: You must LISTEN! When we do not listen, we risk:
- being hobbled by our own assumptions, which may or may not be accurate;
- misunderstanding our students; and/or
- missing the opportunity to enhance instruction.

However, listening is hard to do and must be done with intention.

Level IV: Student Lens Shifts Teacher Lens. At this level, the teacher troubles her or his assumptions about what students know, who they are, and what they can do—and plans for and allows for students to be leaders in the lesson. The teacher is willing to let go of control and to allow the students to make meaningful connections that can then be capitalized upon for instructional purposes. Both the teacher and the students are reflective about what they think, what they do, and how they interact. And those reflections impact their conceptual understanding. In order to do this, they must purposefully examine their own frames for understanding and biases (preconceived ideas about how the world works) in order to reflect on them and perhaps shift them based on their interactions. At this level, the teacher creates opportunities for (and benefits from) the students' increased meta-cognition and agency. The teacher intentionally creates spaces and time for self-reflection to examine beliefs and practice both in the planning process and (for students as well) in lesson activities. The teacher integrates the new knowledge into lessons, changing the curricular framework without losing sight of the instructional goals. This level involves a complex, cyclical, and recursive network of interactions between the teacher, the individual students, and the group. Group interaction informs the teacher's and students' individual reflections, which inform the teacher's and students' individual actions, which inform interaction again, and so on. Teachers and students change attitudes, actions, and understandings based on what they *learn from each other*. Using these four levels of contextualization stimulates the students and teachers to build new knowledge together, knowledge they can then jointly reflect and act on.

Level IV Example: You have created a JPA lesson within your nutrition unit where your JPA is to have your students design a brochure to encourage their peers to eat healthy foods using "My Plate." For your content standard, you have incorporated the National Health Education Standard for 3rd–5th grade *(8.5.1): Encourage others to make positive health choices.* You have included the language goal of *practicing persuasive writing.* Through the JPA lesson you find that some of your children come from countries where the nutritional food groups are categorized differently. Rather than the "Proteins," "Grains," "Fruits/Veggies," and "Fats" that we are accustomed to using, they organize them into "Foods that Help with Digestion," "Foods that give Energy," and "Foods that build Muscle and Bone." You begin to think differently about how knowledge is organized, realizing that what you think of as the "normal" way of organizing concepts is not the only way. You encourage your students to incorporate both ways of thinking in their brochure to encourage healthy eating habits, and in a follow-up activity, ask them to consider other ways that food might be categorized.

Level IV Dangers: This level requires both teachers and students to be willing to reflect and be open to change. If teachers and students resist openness:
  - trust and safe environment may be imperiled;
  - discussions may derail into intransigent argument preventing new learning from occurring; and/or
  - the focus of the instructional goal may be lost.

FOOD FOR THOUGHT

Read the following quotation and the Questions to Consider that follow.

"Everyone that you will ever meet knows something that you don't."
Bill Nye the Science Guy

Questions to Consider

- What does it mean that everyone is an expert in their own life?
- How can we be open to learning what our students know in order to lead them to connect to academic content and success in school?

Getting to Know Your Students: I Am Poems

Getting to know our students is a process that requires patience, trust, and listening. One excellent exercise we have found that can help you in this process (while reinforcing writing as well as listening and speaking skills) is the "I Am" poem. In the "I Am" poem, the writer starts each line with the words "I am" or "I am from." There are many templates available for this exercise that offer cloze passages and prompts that can be used (we have one template on our webpage, coe.uga.edu/directory/latino-achievement, and you can search "I Am Poem" or "I Am From Poem" for various options). Alternatively, you might create your own template based on what you want to learn from your students and what they want to learn about each other. This simple technique can pull out surprising insights as well as factual details as students look inside themselves and reflect. These activities can be done at any time of the year, depending on your instructional goal. But at the beginning of the year, they can be especially helpful in building community and providing the teacher with a plethora of information from students about who they are and what matters to them that can be integrated into future lessons. It can also offer a window into how your students think, as well as provide a unique opportunity for your students to get to know you as their teacher.

Contextualizing lessons for students requires considerable planning and work. In order to make lessons real and relevant for students, teachers must be self-reflective about what we know while being open to listening to what they know. However, through this process, teachers can activate many of the assets students bring with them—tapping into their motivations and aptitudes as well as their background knowledge, content literacy skills, social interaction skills, and home language. When students feel connected to what we are teaching and are utilizing the skills that they bring, they become more engaged in their own learning and are more able and willing to tackle challenging and complex problems with confidence, persistence, and autonomy.

CHALLENGING AND COMPLEX ACTIVITIES

The third pair of voussoir blocks, Challenging and Complex Activities, builds on the previous two building blocks, which focus on activating individual language and background knowledge, and creates a bridge to the last two building blocks, which focus on the group activities of collaboration and conversation. This voussoir is where the teacher designs challenging and complex activities, engaging the students in deep thinking and activating their collective assets.

The Arch system is grounded in Vygotsky's sociocultural theoretical framework, which posits that human learning and cognition are culturally bound and inherently embedded in social interaction rather than strictly individual processes (Kozulin, Gindis, Ageyev, & Miller, 2003). For Vygotsky (1978), social interaction is key to the learning process that leads to cognitive development. The goal of teaching is to move students through their developmental stages, so that students will eventually be able to complete, on their own, those concepts and tasks that at first they can complete only with assistance. But to foster that process, teachers must first identify what their students can do independently (zone of actual development) and what they can do with assistance from others (zone of proximal development). It is in the space between what students can do on their own and what is too difficult for them to do on their own—the zone of proximal development, or ZPD—that learning occurs.

The challenge for teaching is that the ZPD is a moving target that differs for each student and may even differ across subjects and tasks for any particular student. As students develop, their ZPDs move; tasks that were once too hard for them to complete or understand without assistance become tasks that they do independently. Through social interaction and collaboration with others, students participating in JPAs have the opportunity to learn from one another, challenging each other's understanding, and in turn, scaffolding one another's learning (Lantolf et al., 2015). Creating lessons that activate each student's individual ZPD requires knowing your students.

JPA Task Card: Lesson Planning for the ZPD

Instructional Goal

To practice planning lessons considering when and how to use JPAs in a unit plan to promote learning and proficiency.

Task Activities

In your PLC:

- As you are reading the description of the ZPD Chart, imagine that your grade-level team is planning an ELA unit on fairy tales.
- Work together as a group to decide where the Fairy Tale Unit Lesson Ideas described below might fit on the ZPD Chart.
- Discuss with your group what variables would impact where and when you would implement the lessons. Consider the following:
  - » What is your instructional goal with each lesson?
  - » When might you enact them in the unit plan, and why?
  - » What competence do your students have or need to complete this lesson activity?
  - » Would your instructional goal be best met if the lesson were designed as whole-group direct instruction, individual work, or JPAs?

Fairy Tale Unit Lesson Ideas

- Create a Venn diagram comparing and contrasting two versions of Cinderella.
- Identify and outline the main elements of a fairy tale and its structure.
- Write a fairy tale that incorporates all the main elements.
- Read a fairy tale and create a three-column chart identifying the main characters, their character traits, and evidence from the text.
- Write a paragraph with evidence from the text about their character traits arguing if the main characters are admirable or not.
- Review the lists of character traits attributable to the characters. Find evidence for them in the text.

Questions to Consider

- How might your decisions about where the lesson fits on the ZPD chart change with different groups of children?
- How might you plan these lessons so your students might work together to scaffold for one another?
- How did engaging in this activity make you think differently about planning with your students' ZPD in mind? How might this impact your planning in the future?

Figure 5.2. Lesson Planning for the Zone of Proximal Development

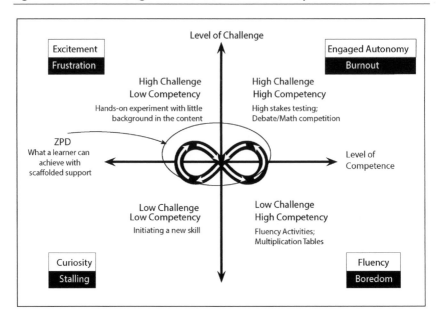

Lesson Planning for the ZPD

We have found in talking with teachers that although many have a strong conceptual understanding of the ZPD, they struggle with how to apply that understanding to the practical activity of lesson planning. Therefore, we have developed a chart (Figure 5.2) for teachers to use as they plan lessons, guiding implementation of the ZPD concept. The vertical axis represents the *Level of Challenge* of the task, with low level of challenge toward the bottom and high level of challenge toward the top. The horizontal axis represents the *Level of Competence* of the student, with low level of competence toward the left and high level of competence toward the right. At the center of the quadrants is the *Zone of Proximal Development*: This is our target.

To help teachers plan with this target in mind, we have placed at the four corners of the chart two anchor words that represent the benefit and challenge inherent to each quadrant. These reminders underscore that each quadrant is important to learning, and teachers should consider planning lessons in each to continuously promote students' development. However, there are dangers to staying in any section for too long. We begin by discussing each quadrant in turn and what kinds of instructional goals might be met by planning a lesson that fits in each. The JPA "Lesson Planning for the ZPD" may help to guide your reflection during the description of the quadrant chart.

Consider, first, the bottom left quadrant. This quadrant represents *Low Level of Competence* and *Low Level of Challenge*. This is where students are initiating a new skill and becoming oriented to their new learning. In learning to swim, this quadrant would be when you are just dipping your toes in, blowing bubbles, learning to float, and getting accustomed to the water. At this stage of learning, you don't have the skills to swim on your own and might be nervous about being in the water. But this step is necessary in order to learn to swim. In the classroom, this quadrant is where a teacher tries to build students' curiosity, introduce a new concept, and make students feel comfortable with starting something new. This quadrant is essential: Introducing new skills is commonplace in school, and should be done in a way that sparks curiosity while establishing the foundational skills and understanding necessary to build mastery. However, if teachers get stuck in this quadrant—if they don't provide opportunities for students to develop competence through practice and by gradually increasing the challenge while releasing control— they run the risk of their students stalling.

But how can we move our students out of this quadrant, to build their excitement about a new skill before they have had the chance to develop competence? The top left corner of the chart represents lessons with a *High Level of Challenge* but where our students have a *Low Level of Competency*. In this quadrant, students can see what is possible if they learn the new skill, which will excite them. Think about the swimming metaphor—this quadrant is where you take students who are learning to swim to a waterpark with a giant water slide. The slide is exciting and can be scary, but they don't need to have strong swimming skills to enjoy it; all they need to do is have the courage to slide down, splash in the water, and paddle to the side. The benefit to this quadrant is that your students can play with the new skill, without having to be an expert. A classroom example might be a beginning unit on circuits: You give your students a box of wires, batteries, and light bulbs, and tell them if they connect them the right way, the light bulbs will light. The students have no idea how circuits work, but you can imagine how excited they will be the first time they manage to get the light bulb to light up! They will have more interest in learning about how circuits work once they have had the chance to play with them. Teachers want to provide opportunities for students to play with new ideas in an exciting way, and to engage them in concepts even before they have achieved a level of competence. Their excitement inspires students to think about what they are learning, ask questions, and want to learn more. Lessons aimed at the top left quadrant push students to the edge of their ZPD, where they will require assistance. But if teachers pitch the activities too high too often, never giving students the chance to become competent in the skill or content, frustration or fear can ensue.

In order to alleviate that fear or frustration, we build competence and confidence through lessons in the lower right quadrant: that of *Low Level of Challenge* with a *High Level of Competency*. Lessons in this quadrant build automaticity—increased speed through accumulated practice. Consider again the swimming metaphor: This quadrant is where students swim laps, do stroke drills, and focus on building resistance, stamina, and skill. In the classroom, low challenge/high competency exercises work on fluency through activities that allow the students' skills to become automatic. These might include such activities as practicing multiplication tables, learning sight words, or reading texts that are familiar or at or below the student's level. To feel confident in their abilities, students must engage in repetitive practice that doesn't present too high a challenge, so they can achieve fluency and feel successful. This success builds confidence. For example, it's a good idea to allow students to choose books for independent reading that are at or below their grade level if they enjoy them; that practice maintains the skills they have developed and helps build fluency, confidence, and delight in learning. Students can be encouraged to read those texts to younger siblings or younger students in the school (this helps both learners). Again, thinking about a student learning to swim, without constant repetitive practice they will not be prepared to compete in high-stakes competitions. Practice and drilling create body memory, so when faced with a high level of challenge the student can meet the challenge with poise because the skills the activity requires have become automatic.

This quadrant differs from the other three in that it does not require the hyperfocus of something new or very challenging. Instead, it calls for the "blurry" focus of patterned, repetitive behavior that allows the mind to rest and recover and to move into a kind of meditative place; this opens doors to creativity and problem-solving. The lower right quadrant has earned a bad reputation in education in recent years because some traditional classrooms focus almost exclusively on "drill and kill" methods that don't necessarily promote complex thinking. However, providing the space for practice and repetition is necessary to help our students build stamina and prepare for greater challenges. Nevertheless, although repetition is good, if students stay too long in this quadrant they risk becoming bored and, more importantly, do not grow and progress.

The activities in the bottom right quadrant help to move students through their ZPD, from what they can do with support to engaged autonomy in their learning. We want them to move to the upper right quadrant where they can confidently meet a *High Level of Challenge* that requires a *High Level of Competency* on their own. This quadrant is where our students test themselves, assessing how far they can stretch. In our swimming metaphor, this is the quadrant where we would have swim meets and competitions to push our students' skills to their limits. In our classrooms, lessons might take the form of summative assessments, debates, performances, and competitions. However, these activities should not be an end in themselves where the "grade" is the goal, but rather a means to see how much students have learned and to build the desire to try and learn more. These activities should be the culminating demonstration of the students' achievement and a satisfying illustration *to the student* of what they are capable of doing on their own. This quadrant, like the three others, is necessary, but cannot be the only place we focus our attention.

Unfortunately, in contemporary schools, it sometimes seems that testing is all teachers do—that the test has become the *raison d'être* of schooling. Under this pressure, teachers tend to plan and teach as though the desired trajectory through the ZPD moves directly from initiating a skill to testing it (bottom left to top right on the chart). But let us not forget that Olympic athletes prepare for the Olympics only every 4 years. Regardless of how accomplished they are in the sport that they love, they would burn out and lose all the joy of participating if they had to compete at that level of challenge every day. So how should we think about planning lessons with this in mind? Each of the quadrants is essential for continued growth, and they all work together. Learning is a recursive process.

Teachers don't want students ever to feel that they have learned all that there is to learn. We want them to be willing to initiate new things and to begin new learning with excitement and confidence for the rest of their lives. Our planning and their learning should therefore resemble an *infinity loop*, going from initiation of a new content or process, to building excitement about learning it, through practice and routinization of the learning, to engaged autonomy and back to learning something new. Learning is a recursive, cyclical process that constantly builds in complexity, but we often think of it as a straight line beginning at point A and *ending* at point B. The journey from novice to mastery should be an exciting never-ending process where, with practice and innovation, learners are constantly integrating new skills and ideas.

However, think about "gifted" students who often are hesitant to try a new thing because they are afraid of failing or of not being good at the new skill from the very beginning. Consider how to create a classroom where beginning a new skill feels safe and exciting. Recognize that a certain amount of practice is necessary to help students arrive at the point where they can be accomplished and autonomous (and be tested for their skills). And remember, the ZPD *should* be constantly changing for every student, in every subject, every day because they're learning and growing.

The challenge for teachers is to plan for this growth intentionally, integrating activities in unit plans in all four quadrants, giving students the tools to become autonomous learners. Our hope is that by using this ZPD chart to intentionally plan lessons that fit in each quadrant, teachers can go a long way toward meeting our collective goal of creating independent learners who are not afraid to try something new, are excited about learning, have the determination and discipline to practice their skills, and take pleasure in testing their abilities to their limits.

Productive Struggle

Testing those limits promotes deep and complex thinking that requires challenging mental processes such as hypothesizing, testing, evaluating, and synthesizing information. These processes take hard work and can sometimes be a struggle—a struggle which we as teachers may find hard to simply stand back and watch. Wanting to help is not a bad thing—it's why many of us became teachers in the first place. The question is how to help students so that they can grow and become independent in their learning. If we give students the answer and they don't have to struggle to arrive at it on their own, they won't build the mental muscles necessary to be able to do it again. We must allow our students to struggle productively. Robin Jackson and Claire Lambert (2010) discuss the difference between productive and destructive struggle, as outlined in Table 5.3.

By creating lessons that are within the students' ZPD and providing them with tools to productively collaborate and scaffold for one another, we can ensure that our students can confront complex and challenging tasks with confidence and perseverance, while positively contributing to each other's learning.

Note About Collaboration and Conversation: The Last Two Pairs of Voussoirs

In the preceding chapters and sections we have been building the Arch of Collaborative, Conversation-Based Instruction, exploring in detail each of the Arch elements: beginning at the foundation and moving up the columns and through the first three pairs of voussoirs. We have now arrived at *collaboration* and *conversation*, the final two pairs of voussoirs in the Arch system. The Arch builds to these blocks; however, the rationale for why collaboration and conversation positively impact learning permeates the entire text. Similarly, the tools and strategies necessary to facilitate productive collaboration and conversation in JPA lessons are embedded in every chapter. Therefore, the following two sections don't cover all the ways collaboration

Table 5.3. Destructive vs. Productive Struggle

A Destructive Struggle	A Productive Struggle
Leads to frustration	Leads to understanding
Makes learning goals feel hazy and out of reach	Makes learning goals feel attainable and effort seem worthwhile
Feels fruitless	Yields results
Leaves students feeling abandoned and on their own	Leads students to feelings of empowerment and efficacy
Creates a sense of inadequacy	Creates a sense of hope

and conversation can be supported and implemented in the classroom. Instead, they focus on two targeted strategies. In the section on collaboration, we look at how to support peer scaffolding to promote productive collaboration; and in the section on conversation, we discuss how to use experiential stories to make conversations more engaging, memorable, and connected to academic learning.

COLLABORATION

When discussing the first three pairs of voussoirs in the Arch system and how they interact to activate the assets everyone brings to the classroom, we have focused largely on the teacher side of the Arch and what the *teacher* does to plan and implement lessons—integrating language and literacy goals, contextualizing for meaning, and maintaining complexity and challenge. It's important to note that we have been building the supports necessary for collaboration throughout the text; many keys to creating opportunities for our students to work collaboratively lie in establishing a safe environment and providing scaffolding tools (which we discussed in Chapters 2 and 4). These tools—norms, sentence starters, goal cards, etc.—are crucial to opening space and giving our students what they need to be able to collaborate with each other successfully. Furthermore, the importance of purposeful planning cannot be overstated. Intentional planning, both in the organization of classrooms and the structure of lessons, is key for collaboration to happen. But as teachers plan JPAs—collaborative group lessons—they must be mindful that just having students work in small groups does not guarantee collaboration. So as we discuss the fourth pair of voussoir blocks, we will focus more heavily on what the *students* can do to collaborate productively. We will concentrate on the role of carefully and intentionally planned JPAs as spaces for collaboration and peer scaffolding that allow each member of

---

NOTES FROM THE FIELD

Consider the vignette and the questions that follow.

Last spring, we were invited to observe a 1st-grade teacher conduct a JPA on short and long vowels. She and the four boys she had chosen for this JPA were seated facing each other around a table. In the center of the table were a stack of pictures with different familiar objects such as a cat, a gate, a boat, a pot, etc. and two labels that read "Short Vowel" and "Long Vowel." One by one, the boys selected cards from the stack, discussed the pictures, and sorted the cards under the labels according to whether the object represented had a short or long vowel.

A sandy-haired boy in a Spiderman T-shirt held up a card with a picture of a cat on it, and sharply nodding his head said confidently, "I think this is a short vowel because 'cat' sounds like /æ/." At one point, the sandy-haired boy moved to put the card with the cat on it under the label marked "Short Vowels" and then paused. Drawing his hand back and looking at the other three boys in his group, he asked, "Do you agree?" Two of his companions immediately nodded in affirmation and said, "I agree." But the third, a round-faced boy with dark hair and blue eyes, didn't answer. A look of consternation on his face, he shifted his gaze back and forth from the card to the labels laid out on the table. The first boy waited a moment and then asked him, "What do you think, Randall?"

Biting his bottom lip slightly, a wrinkle creasing the space between his eyebrows, Randall responded, "I'm still thinking about your answer, Sam. Tell me about your reasoning."

We were staggered by Randall's response. Here was a 6-year-old asking another 6-year-old to explain his reasoning! *Who was this gifted child interacting with his peers and probing them like a teacher?* We scooted to the edge of our seats, excited to hear more.

Sam looked down at the card, and then, glancing at the other boys as if for support said, "Well, I think it's a short vowel, because it doesn't have an 'e' on the end. What do you think, Jackson?"

The slight, brown-skinned boy seated to Sam's left chimed in, "I agree it's a short vowel. This morning, Ms. W. said that words with the 'magic e' usually have long vowels! Remember?" At that, he smiled widely, showing a gap where his two front teeth had been.

As Sam held up the card for Randall to see, we noticed that the card had only the picture of a cat, but no words. Randall must have noticed this too, because he asked, "How did you know it doesn't have an 'e'?" At that, both Sam and Jackson turned, pointing to the word wall behind them where there was a picture of a cat with CAT written under it, and in chorus responded, "We used our resources!" At that, Randall nodded sagely, head cocked to one side and said, "Yes, I agree, it is a short vowel."

NOTES FROM THE FIELD, CONTINUED

After the lesson we talked with Mrs. W. and were astounded to find out that Randall was not only not in the gifted program, but had an IEP. Ms. W. had put him in this JPA group with Sam and Jackson so that he could have extra modeling and scaffolded support. But Randall wasn't the only one who gained from this grouping; the scaffolding was reciprocal. Because the boys had the tools they needed—both material (pictures, word wall), and linguistic (question stems, semi-preconstructed conversational moves such as "Tell me about your reasoning," etc.)—they were able to support each other. Randall had the conceptual reasoning and language modeled for him and demonstrated in several ways to help deepen his understanding, while the other two boys had to do mental gymnastics to think of other ways to "explain their reasoning." Everyone benefited, while no one felt singled out or put upon.

Questions to Consider

- What scaffolding supports did Sam and Jackson offer Randall?
- What scaffolding supports did Randall offer Sam and Jackson?
- How can intentional grouping impact collaboration so that all students' needs are met?

the group to benefit from the interaction, make meaningful connections, practice language, and solve complex problems.

All of us have heard of (if not lived through!) terrible group-work experiences that do not meet the principle goal of collaboration—to multiply the skills and talents each individual brings to the table to creatively solve complex problems—but instead devolve into frustrating experiences that can actually inhibit learning rather than promote it (Oakley, Felder, Brent, & Elhajj, 2004). While the benefits of collaborative work for both cognitive and social development have been shown in many studies (Olsen & Finkelstein, 2017; Rickel & Johnson, 2000; Teasley, 1997; Webb et al., 2017), students are not born with the skills necessary for effective group work; they must be given the tools to listen effectively, to ask good questions, to synthesize and build off others' ideas, and to disagree productively (Kuhn, 2015). Once armed with these tools, they must be given ample and regular opportunities to *reflect* on their own strengths and challenges and to *practice* using the tools of collaboration. In this way, effective collaboration becomes a habit, and positive, productive interaction with peers becomes automatic.

**JPA Task Card: Collaboration and Peer Scaffolding
as Tools for Learning**

Contextualization

Damian, Rachel, Amad, and Sofia are working collaboratively in a JPA. The task is to respond to a document-based question about two passages: one about Frederick Douglass and one about Abraham Lincoln. They must work together to write a constructed response discussing three similarities and three differences between the two men, supported by evidence from the texts.

Instructional Goal

To examine how students can scaffold for one another and collaborate to accomplish together what they couldn't do alone.

Task Activities

In your PLC:

- Read and discuss the transcript of Sofia, Ahmad, Damian, and Rachel's conversation shown below:

Rachel: Okay, the question says, "How are Frederick Douglass and Abraham Lincoln the same?" So first we rewrite the question, "They were the same because . . . "

Sofia: No, not *they,* "*Frederick Douglass* and *Abraham Lincoln* were the same because . . . " we need to use their names, not just the pronoun. [pause] . . . Because why? [Sofia looks at the text tracing the lines with her fingers]

Rachel: What do you think?

Sofia: Because . . . they both were poor and didn't go to school.

Ahmad: Okay, where do you see that?

Sofia: Here, look [pointing to the text] it says "Lincoln, born dirt poor, had less than a year of formal schooling. Douglass, born a slave, wasn't permitted to go to school."

Ahmad: Yeah, okay, that's good, and . . . ah! . . look for the word "both" . . . they were *both* famous around the world.

Damian: How did you get that they're famous?

Rachel: [points to the passage and reads] "They both rose to international prominence."

Damian: Prominence is famous?

Rachel: Yeah, prominence—like *prominencia,* in Spanish or *prominente,* prominent.

JPA Task Card: Collaboration and Peer Scaffolding as Tools for Learning, continued

Damian: Ah . . . yeah . . . but I wonder, I mean, isn't that more like like *curvas prominentes*? "prominent curves"—You know, like the Kardashians? [Damian moves his hands in an hour-glass shape. The students laugh.]

Rachel: Yeah, I see what you mean, but I think it can be both . . . I don't think Lincoln had prominent curves! [pause] What's e-emancipated? [pronouncing the word emanCIpated]

Sofia: eMANcipated? I think it means like liberated—you know, *emancipado,* emancipated. Let me look it up. [opens dictionary and leafs through] Yeah, emancipate, like *liberado,* means "to liberate" or "to set free."

Damian: Sí, okay, that makes sense. [repeats softly] *liberado* . . . liberate.

Rachel: So, let's put that they both wanted to liberate the slaves.

Ahmad: Good one! Should we say liberate or emancipate?

Rachel: I think both are okay—but maybe we write emancipate because of the Emancipation Proclamation—it's like it goes more with slavery? [pause while Sofia writes] Okay now we need the differences. [Damian sighs]

Ahmad: Come on, we can do this! [taps on the text] We're almost done!

- Work together, making sure you hear from all members of your group.
- Create a three-column chart.
- In the *first column* identify specific evidence of how the students scaffold for each other to support their learning.
- In the *second column* indicate if the scaffolding tool is:
  » linguistic—using language as tools; e.g., modeling, recasting, comparing to other languages, gestures, etc.
  » material—using physical tools like the text, dictionaries, manipulatives
  » heuristic—using "shortcuts" like educated guesses, assumptions based on background knowledge, stereotypes, mnemonic devices, etc.
- In the *third column*, explain your thoughts about what they are accomplishing with this scaffold.

**JPA Task Card: Collaboration and Peer Scaffolding
as Tools for Learning, continued**

Questions to Consider

- How do the students access and activate their individual assets to help each other learn new content?
- How can the teacher impact this process?
- What assets can our students use as tools to scaffold for each other that may not be available to us as teachers?
- How can we recognize and support when our students are scaffolding for each other?

Collaboration Is About Consensus NOT About Competition

For some, working in groups can be a highly emotionally charged endeavor, framed more like a competition, where students are constantly striving to beat the other students and show that they know the answer. For others, this same situation can cause terrible anxiety and drive them to shut down, act out, or give up. To achieve successful collaborative conversations and reach consensus, students must step away from the goal of "winning." This is hard to do, particularly when people feel very strongly about something or when they feel like their self-worth hinges upon being right. But collaboration isn't about who talks louder or more eloquently or more persuasively; sometimes the quietest participant has the best answer to meet the group's goals. True collaboration is about *listening* and *synthesis* and *compromise* and *change*.

Three underlying assumptions are critical to successful JPAs, and both teachers and students must be aware of them: (1) The voice of every member of the group matters; (2) Every person in the group brings with them experience, knowledge, and understanding that can benefit the group; and (3) The goal of collaboration is to seek the best answer/strategy/process to address *this* problem in *this* context, capitalizing on the strengths of *this* group, not necessarily to find a universally right answer. To reach this collaborative goal, each member of the group must exercise self-reflection and be willing to both listen and share, while being open to change.

Joint Productive Activities are an invaluable tool to facilitate this process because they help move even the most controversial issues from the subjective/affective (where they can be charged with emotion) into a more objective/cognitive realm. JPAs allow groups to put each of the group members' ideas on the table (literally) so that everyone can see them and move them around. This distancing not only facilitates individuals' seeing and considering others' ideas, but also makes it easier to objectively view and consider one's own ideas without feeling personally judged. At the end of the process there may still be some things that the group does not agree upon, and that's okay. Disagreement can sponsor healthy dialogue and positive change, but through true collaboration, group members learn from each other and can come to agreement on the best way to progress for the betterment of the whole group. Tools for listening, habits of collaboration, and norms for conversation become pivotal because they sponsor self-reflection, self-regulation, and mindfulness of our peers (see Chapters 2 and 4). As we think about how teachers can provide students with spaces and tools for collaboration, let us also consider how our students can use collaborative interactions to scaffold for one another and support each other's learning.

Collaboration and Peer Scaffolding

Collaboration provides the space for scaffolding, which helps make collaboration more productive because it capitalizes on the strengths of everyone in the group. The idea of scaffolding as a metaphor in education was introduced by Bruner (1975) and is firmly grounded in the Vygotskian premise that learning is linked to collaborative interaction and mediated through tools or props (i.e., scaffolds) (Walqui, 2006). When people collaborate with others, we participate in communities of practice and apprentice into new ways of thinking (Wenger & Lave, 2001). As a group talks through problems, members provide different insights or strategies for arriving at a solution and can help the group to understand concepts in ways no member could achieve alone (Lantolf et al., 2015). While scaffolded interactions have traditionally been understood to reflect an expert–novice relationship (i.e., teacher–student or parent–child), recent studies suggest that effective scaffolding can take place in pairs or small groups of peers to promote multiliteracy, and that the positive impacts of collaboration are not unidirectional, but reciprocal—that is, both parties in the collaboration benefit rather than one facilitating the learning of the other (Kirova & Jamison, 2018; Ranjbar & Ghonsooly, 2017). These reciprocal scaffolding relationships can be facilitated by the use of tools. We have grouped various scaffolding tools into three broad categories to help us talk about what they are and how they can be used. We hope these descriptions will help you identify and model them in your classrooms, so that your students may begin to use them intentionally to scaffold for their peers as they collaborate in JPAs.

Linguistic scaffolds are tools that use language to help students understand a concept more clearly or to encourage, redirect, or engage them in the task. Linguistic scaffolds might include tools such as questioning/

listening, modeling, recasting, the use of norms for collaboration, semi-preconstructed phrases, conversation starters, etc. Linguistic scaffolds might also include paralinguistic features like gestures, facial expressions, and changes in intonation or stress that are used to call a conversation partner's attention to something that needs to be addressed or changed. For example, when students are collaborating in a JPA they can use the same kinds of corrective feedback strategies teachers use to scaffold for each other and heighten metalinguistic awareness (see the corrective feedback chart, Table 5.2). They can model language or concepts and recast when another student misuses or mispronounces words. They can use sentence stems to promote collaboration and invite their peers into the conversation.

Material scaffolds are physical tools used to support learning by offering visible, maneuverable examples that students can see and manipulate. Material scaffolding tools may include manipulatives, pictures or graphics, realia, texts, task cards, goal cards, dictionaries, multimedia sources, other reference tools, etc. JPAs are material scaffolds almost by definition—that is, they provide physical scaffolds in the form of a task card and a tangible product that the students can manipulate and collaborate to complete. Students can use material scaffolds to collaborate with their peers even when they don't yet have the language to converse fluently. While teachers can prepare material scaffolds such as cloze passages, graphics, and descriptions, students can reference texts, employ dictionaries, and create or point to visual examples. They can also use manipulatives or other realia to build models and examples to illustrate their thinking to their peers, thereby helping them to see from different perspectives as they collaborate to solve a problem.

Finally, *heuristic scaffolds* are "tricks of the trade" that help with decision making and memory by providing mental shortcuts that reduce the cognitive load (Collins, Brown, & Newman, 1989). These abstract tools can be useful as both intuitive and deliberate mental strategies because they capitalize on the brain's tendency to look for simple efficient rules to solve complex problems (Kruglanski & Gigerenzer, 2018). Heuristic scaffolds can include such tools as stereotyping, educated guesses, working backward, mnemonic devices, metaphors, references to background knowledge or popular culture, etc. For example, if a group of students was collaborating in a JPA finding evidence for the themes of love vs. duty in *Romeo and Juliet*, they might scaffold for each other's understanding by referencing a popular television program like *Game of Thrones* or *Empire*. They might also include cross-linguistic comparisons (see Hardmeier, 2015) and multi-sensory connections like connecting words with music.

Teachers can facilitate peer scaffolding by making students aware of different scaffolding tools available to them and creating JPAs that afford them the space and time to practice scaffolding and assisting each other in moving through their ZPDs. The productive collaboration that JPAs foster can help students access and activate their own resources as well as each other's. Furthermore, because students come with different assets (social interaction skills, background knowledge, home language, etc.) there are scaffolds our students can employ for each other that we do not have access to. We may not immediately be able to see how the students are helping each other. However, we must take the time to examine what our students are doing and recognize how they scaffold for each other—even if they are using tools that are unfamiliar or unavailable to us. By teaching our students how to deliberately use scaffolds, we increase our students' autonomy in their learning and their ability to transfer that learning to the task of addressing real-world problems both in and outside the classroom environment.

PURPOSEFUL CONVERSATION

The final pair of voussoirs in the Arch system—the one that frames the keystone of the Joint Productive Activity—represents conversation. This trio of voussoir blocks and keystone forms the apex of the Arch for a reason; the blocks are both the culmination of, and the means to unite, every block of the Arch that comprises the structure. The conversation voussoirs and the keystone support and promote one another, creating a balanced force. Just as the JPA gives structure and purpose to conversation, conversation elevates the JPA from being a simple group task to being something greater. The purposeful conversations that support JPAs are not simply conversation for conversation's sake; they provide students with authentic opportunities to build language skills by listening to and interacting with their peers, and to make meaningful connections to the content concepts they are learning.

When you examine the Arch graphic, you see that the paired goals of the conversation voussoirs are *learning* through purposeful conversation on the students' side and *teaching* through purposeful conversation on the teacher's side. While this may seem basic, this reciprocal relationship is fundamental to the system's integrity. It means that when students have the structure to talk through their thinking as they complete a shared task, they tell stories from their lives, connecting what they know and building off each other's ideas. This helps them to create profound and lasting connections to new information. One of the teacher's roles in this complex dance

JPA Task Card: Experiential Stories and Purposeful Conversation as Tools for Learning

Instructional Goal

To examine how we can connect our stories to academic content through guided reflection and purposeful conversation.

Task Activities

With your PLC:

- Consider the Notes from the Field, Food for Thought, and JPA boxes you read and engaged in throughout the book.
- Reference your journal entries and any notes or artifacts that you created as you completed these activities with your PLCs.
- Discuss the connections you and your peers made, and the stories you exchanged to explain and connect your thinking while engaging in these activities.
- Create a four-column flow chart with the following headings: (1) Title/Topic, (2) Text, (3) Story, (4) Purposeful Conversation
- Together discuss and fill out the chart:
  » Column 1: Look back over the various Food for Thought, Notes from the Field or JPA boxes and write their Titles/Topics.
  » Column 2: Indicate a point or example from the text that provoked a connection (to another text, to self, to world) for your group members.
  » Column 3: Describe one or more stories summarizing the personal connection you and the members of your PLC made to the example in column 2.
  » Column 4: Describe how conversing with your PLC about these connections changed or expanded your thinking about the overall idea or problem presented in the box.

Questions to Consider

- How can the stories we tell each other to explain and connect our experiences impact our ability to integrate new knowledge?
- How do the Questions to Consider help us to connect what we know (framed through the stories we tell) to new learning?
- How can we use tools like the scenarios and journals to promote purposeful conversations that connect our students' experiences to our instructional goals?

NOTES FROM THE FIELD: CONNECTING OUR STORIES THROUGH CONVERSATION

Consider the following scenario and the questions to consider.

An 8th-grade ELA teacher and an 8th-grade social studies teacher co-planned a JPA that used the current events example of the "tri-state water wars" litigation case as a means to teach "point of view" (an 8th-grade ELA standard) and "the importance of water in Georgia's historical development and economic growth" (an 8th-grade social studies standard). These abstract concepts are hard for students to grasp or relate to, so the teachers make them more accessible and memorable by creating a JPA that allowed the students to wrestle with the ideas while connecting them to their own experiences.

The day of the JPA, the students were given four newspaper articles about the upcoming Supreme Court decision determining who has the right to the water from two major river basins that originate north of Atlanta. Because the instructional goal was point of view, one article was from the *Tampa Bay Times*, one from the Montgomery *Advertiser*, one from the Atlanta *Journal-Constitution* and one from the *Washington Post*.

The students were asked to create a T-Chart identifying the various stakeholders in the case and offering evidence from the text of why they were fighting for the water rights. They were asked to use this chart to propose a plan for how the water could be fairly used. When we came to the class, a group of four students was working collaboratively on this task. The following is an excerpt from their conversation:

> *D'Asia:* Okay, so Georgia, Florida, and Alabama are the ones taking the case to the Supreme Court.
>
> *Wei:* Yes, that's true, but this article [pointing to the Atlanta *Journal-Constitution*] says that the *farmers* are fighting for the water.
>
> *Susana:* Farmers? Why farmers?
>
> *Wei:* It says here that the farmers lost their crops during the last drought. They say the people in Atlanta used up the water before it could go down the river and get to them.
>
> *Carlo:* Yeah, that's why we came to live up here. I grew up down in Early County. My parents worked on the cotton farms, but during the drought, the plants all died—the farmer couldn't pay the workers and we had to move.
>
> *Susana:* Wow, that's wack. I would hate to leave my home. At least you came to Atlanta where we have the water!
>
> *D'Asia:* Yeah, but for how long? Remember last year when you couldn't wash your car. My dad used to go outside and water the grass in the middle of the night!

NOTES FROM THE FIELD: CONNECTING OUR STORIES THROUGH CONVERSATION,
CONTINUED

Wei: And the more people that come here, the worse it will be for the people in South Georgia and Florida.

Teacher: So how should the Supreme Court decide who gets to use the water? How does where you live impact your point of view about this?

Susana: Hmm. I think it would matter a lot. I mean my mom used to hate not being able to wash the car, but we didn't have to move!

Teacher: And Wei, you mentioned that more people are moving to Atlanta and that will be worse for people downriver. What do you mean by that?

Wei: Well, they will have less water if more people are using water in Atlanta.

Teacher: And what kinds of impacts might that have on people in Atlanta?

Carlo: There will be more people moving here because they don't have work!

After the JPA, the teacher debriefed the lesson to ensure that her goals of understanding point of view and the economic impact of water on Georgia's economic growth were met.

Questions to Consider

- How did the students sharing their stories, building off each others' ideas in conversation, help the students connect more deeply to the content?
- How did this process help the teacher meet her instructional goals of their learning point of view and the impact of water on Georgia's economic growth?
- What role did the teacher play in the lesson?

is to provide opportunities for purposeful conversation through JPAs—creating a space and a reason for students to talk and share their stories. Furthermore, the teacher's role in posing thoughtful and responsive questions enables students to activate not only their background knowledge, but also their embodied knowledge, creating a gateway to deeper understanding that they can transfer and apply to collaboratively address complex problems.

Throughout the text, we have discussed at length various ways to support productive conversation in classrooms, but in this section, we want to pull out and focus on a single idea: that stories—the way people talk about lived experience—can be a catalyst for conversation, foster connections to each other and the content, and elevate instruction.

It is not uncommon to think of storytelling as a pastime based on imaginative fictions: an act where we invent and create worlds that don't exist, for our own and others' entertainment. The term "storytelling" may evoke the image of a person sitting in a chair, regaling a group of rapt listeners with a tale—and while that may be one kind of storytelling, it comprises a much larger part of our social existence. People often tell stories to frame or contextualize their experience and make sense of their world. We use stories in all aspects of our lives to instruct, to inform, to relate, but also simply to communicate and connect within our social landscape. We tell stories to explain the past, interpret the present, and predict the future. When we engage in conversation, through the exchange of our stories, we show how we think and why we think it. By harnessing the power of stories with students in the classroom through *purposeful* conversations, teachers can begin to develop mutual understanding and create stronger communities of practice that can allow teachers and students to interpret and solve problems together.

Research at the intersection of cognitive psychology, neurolinguistics, and artificial intelligence suggests that knowledge organization is schematic in nature and all knowledge is constructed through "stories" or schemata of associated episodes in our minds (Schank & Abelson, 1995). These schemata (similar to the semi-preconstructed phrases, collocations, and adjacency pairs discussed in Chapter 3) work like a storyboard for familiar situations: a framework of features or ideas that happen in an expected order making the situation easier to understand and negotiate (Mandler, 2014). Stories facilitate predictions of what will happen next (based on what we have already seen or understood) and make it easier for us to make decisions and move through life without having to think too hard. Memory is stored, retrieved, communicated to others, and applied to new experiences through these stories (Schank & Abelson, 1995).

To help explain how stories can be used to support instruction, we'd like to focus for a moment on the interactive activities that you have engaged in as you read the text. As you know, we have included three types of interactive activities throughout the text to guide you as you read: *Notes from the Field* (stories that help connect the ideas we are trying to convey to what is familiar to you as teachers); *Food for Thought* (quotations that highlight specific themes); and *JPAs* (tasks designed for interaction and collaboration). The questions to consider in the Notes from the Field and Food for Thought boxes are designed to help you focus your reflections on the scenarios (stories). The questions in the JPAs are planned to promote rich conversation that sparks connections with the content, each other, and your own experience. The JPA Experiential Stories and Purposeful Conversation as Tools for Learning will help to debrief these interactive activities and unpack the power of stories in learning."

We hope that you now have a clearer idea of how stories connect us to our learning from having experienced and examined it. As you reflect on the power of storytelling, consider how you can apply the concepts of storytelling and purposeful conversation to your classroom. To activate our students' assets, it is important that we ask students questions that prompt them to connect their knowledge to lived experience and talk about it. When teachers ask students a question such as "What is your definition of sequencing?" their response will likely demonstrate what they *think* about the term and what it means. Such an answer is difficult to remember, is devoid of meaningful context and detail, can generate fragmentation, and is often incongruent with personal knowledge and experience. However, if you ask someone to describe *an example of* sequencing *from their experience* and to use that example to explain and define sequencing, their response is likely to be connected to real life and to prompt them to incorporate sensory imagery related to that lived experience. For that reason, "stories" are memorable (both to the speaker and to the listener) and provide ways to connect and apply that lived experience in other contexts (Schank & Abelson, 1995). As students collaborate in JPAs and engage in purposeful conversation to address a shared problem, the stories generated through their discussion can illuminate subtle moments of learning and insight, and reveal what they know without knowing it—allowing intuitive, unconscious, and unexpected connections to emerge. Through JPAs and well-placed questions, teachers can facilitate students' identifying patterns and themes from seemingly disconnected situations and experiences, and support them to intentionally and consciously apply tools, insights, and frameworks learned in one place to other situations.

By means of purposeful conversation, conversation that has the structured focus of the JPA task and its questions, students are able to relate stories from their own experience to meet the instructional goals of the task. Through intentional questions, the teacher can guide the students to a deeper and more meaningful understanding of both specific topics or problems and the overarching instructional goals that can then be transferred to future learning. So when we say we suggest you cultivate storytelling in your classroom, we're not saying that you pull out picture books every time you want to plan a JPA lesson (although there is definitely a space for that!). We're saying that teachers should show students how to relate what they are thinking in coherent narratives—stories—that access their lived experience and *through the process of conversation* explore with their peers how to apply this knowledge to the new problems they are trying to solve.

In the next chapter we will examine the role of the JPA, the keystone to the Arch system, in giving structure and focus to our instructional conversations. We will delve more deeply into how to plan these lessons to support students' purposeful conversation and collaboration and the unique role that the teacher plays.

CHAPTER 6

Placing the Keystone
Designing the Joint Productive Activity (JPA)

Perhaps the most important block in any arch is the keystone—the central block that joins the arch's two sides and holds the whole structure together. In the Arch system for collaborative, conversation-based instruction, the keystone is the Joint Productive Activity (JPA). We have talked in previous chapters about the assets teachers and students bring to the classroom and the importance of activating them through focused and intentional language and literacy development, contextualization, complex activities, and collaborative conversation. These are essential to students' development but, as we have said, the voussoirs would fall down and the columns would never meet to form an integrated whole without the keystone in place.

The JPA is where students are engaged in purposeful conversation, working together to produce a shared product. As you have read through the previous chapters, you have engaged in JPAs with your PLCs and experienced for yourself the power of structured collaborative conversations. We are now going to activate that embodied knowledge so you can apply it to crafting and implementing robust JPAs in your classroom.

Trying something new can be scary, and becoming skilled at creating JPAs that truly capitalize on both teacher and student assets in order to elevate student learning takes considerable practice. This chapter is devoted to discussing the practical details of JPA lesson-planning and the various ways they can be implemented in the classroom. Over the next pages we provide tools and opportunities to practice the following: (1) analyzing the difference between an Independent-JPA and an IC-JPA; (2) deconstructing and planning JPAs; (3) exploring grouping considerations as you begin using JPAs in your classroom; and (4) reflecting on how the Arch system, when implemented in a classroom, can truly join teacher and student assets into a single unified whole.

FOOD FOR THOUGHT

A quotation by a 5th-grade student: "JPAs let you think outside your brain."

Questions to Consider

- How can JPAs promote deep critical thinking that can be applied to complex problems?
- How does "thinking outside your brain" help students to develop their ideas and deepen their understanding of concepts?
- How might JPAs promote a safe space to share ideas and take risks?
- How might having to create a collaborative, tangible product slow down the process and allow space for all students, but especially CLD learners, to participate more fully?

THE JPA:
THE KEYSTONE THAT HOLDS THE ARCH SYSTEM TOGETHER

The Joint Productive Activity (JPA) truly unifies all the voussoirs and makes it possible for teacher and student assets to support one another to achieve shared goals. For practical purposes, the JPA is what it sounds like: a 20–30 minute *activity*, with a clear instructional goal, where a group of 3–7 students work *jointly* through conversation to produce a collective *product*. The JPA task should be complex enough to produce deep thinking and productive conversation; to accomplish this, we suggest creating activities that have either multiple solutions or ways to arrive at a solution (see Chapter 5).

The *product* in the JPA gives the activity structure and focus and is a key factor distinguishing the Arch system from other conversation-based pedagogies (e.g., Socratic method, Harkness model, etc.); it elevates the lesson from being just a "good discussion." Because JPAs have a tangible product, they allow students to literally see their (and others') thoughts and move them around. The act of making students' thinking visible also slows down the collaborative process and allows CLD learners, as well as those students who are less verbal, to participate in the activity even if they don't yet have the oral language or fluency to do so quickly. Furthermore, having a tangible product that the students must complete increases accountability among the group members and allows the teacher to see the students' thinking, offering a simple way to assess participation and understanding.

Lastly, as the Keystone of the Arch system, the JPA joins the other blocks of the arch together and provides students with a structured space: to

Figure 6.1. Types of JPAs: Independent-JPA (left) and IC-JPA (right)

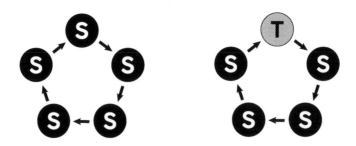

use, practice, and model *language* in a low-stakes environment; to contextualize their knowledge and understanding by making meaningful and relevant *connections* to their lives; to think critically about content, and puzzle through *complex concepts*; and to deepen their understanding (and sharpen their SEL skills) through engaged, productive *collaboration* and purposeful *conversation* with others.

While all JPAs have the same basic components—20–30 minutes, a clear instructional goal, a group of 3–7 students discussing and collaborating to produce a collective product—there are two different kinds of JPAs (Figure 6.1):

- Independent-JPAs—where student groups work independently and the students scaffold for each other within the group, without the teacher continuously present to facilitate; and
- IC-JPAs—where the teacher is continuously present to facilitate and scaffold for the students, enhancing students' engagement with the task.

Independent-JPAs: Where Student Groups Work Independently and Scaffold for Each Other

In simple terms, in an Independent-JPA students work together autonomously on a task with a clear instructional goal that is outlined on a JPA task card, without a teacher's ongoing assistance. The teacher may come by to check in periodically, to ask a probing question, and to make sure there are no major misconceptions; but an Independent-JPA is pitched at a level where students can generally complete the activity with only the peers in their group to scaffold for them. For this reason, it is critical that your students have built the trust, confidence, and skills necessary to collaborate productively without the teacher facilitating and scaffolding before initiating Independent-JPAs. (See Chapter 2 for more on establishing a Safe Foundation and Chapter 4 for more on Scaffolding.)

There are good reasons for implementing Independent-JPAs in any classroom, and we have found that they can be particularly strategic in middle and high school classes, where issues of time and quantity of content present unique limitations. Nonetheless, we do not recommend that teachers implement Independent-JPAs exclusively. The power of integrating successful Independent-JPAs, where students are working collaboratively in independent groups, lies in two main advantages. Independent-JPAs (1) multiply the teacher's instructional time because the students are scaffolding for each other; and (2) afford the teacher the opportunity to work intensively with, and focus on the needs of, one group of students, in what we call an Instructional Conversation, or IC-JPA.

IC-JPAs: Where Teachers Add Value

If you look at the Keystone in the Arch diagram you will notice that the JPA block is divided into two sections, with the narrower portion darker in color. The color is darker because while the JPA is the keystone that holds the collaborative, conversation-based instructional system together, the IC-JPA where the teacher is present serves a special purpose. *IC-JPAs intensify the power of the JPA.* A teacher present with the group of students for the entire 20- to 30-minute lesson can enhance learning by facilitating discussion, increasing the complexity, and differentiating for individual needs. *IC-JPAs provide a low-stakes environment* where the teacher has unparalleled opportunities to formatively assess students, identify and address students' misconceptions as they arise, provide corrective feedback, and model vocabulary. *IC-JPAs afford the teacher the opportunity to get to know students*; by listening deeply to how the students interact and discuss the content, teachers can gain invaluable insight into how they think, what their strengths and challenges are, and what they already know. What they learn can then be used and applied to future lessons. Teachers' presence in the IC-JPA allows them to enhance the impact of each of the other building blocks that comprise the Arch system and support the keystone.

Although teachers sometimes have concerns about the amount of time an IC-JPA can take (20 minutes can seem like a LOT of time to spend with just one group of 3–7 students!), it is time well spent because teachers can strategically plan future lessons that better differentiate for individual student needs because they will have a clearer idea of what those needs are.

JPA TASK CARD: THE IMPACT OF THE TEACHER IN INDEPENDENT-JPAS VS. IC-JPAS

Instructional Goal

To analyze the impact of the teacher in an IC-JPA and what is necessary to promote student interaction.

Task Activities

- Create a Venn diagram, labeling one side Independent-JPA and the other side IC-JPA.
- Read the vignette of the 5th-grade Independent-JPAs and IC-JPA:

In a classroom we recently visited, a 5th-grade teacher was implementing a JPA lesson integrating social studies and ELA standards. They had been studying the Holocaust and World War II and had also read Lois Lowry's *Number the Stars*. For this lesson, the teacher had given the students two pictures, both of children behind barbed wire fences, but one with several dark-haired children dressed in woolen caps and striped pajamas in a German concentration camp, and the other of three adolescent boys dressed in flannel shirts and dark pants in a Japanese internment camp in California. For the JPA, the students were to examine the pictures of the children and create a T-chart detailing the similarities and differences, using descriptive adjectives. The whole class was participating in the same JPA activity, either in Independent-JPA centers around the room, or in one small group with the teacher in an IC-JPA.

Throughout the classroom the students looked at each other as they spoke, easily and organically took turns making sure everyone participated, and really listened to and added to each other's reasoning. We heard them using such language as, "I respectfully disagree with you because . . ." and, as-toundingly, "I hear what you are saying, but let me tell you what I'm thinking . . ." as they compared and discussed the photographs. We were amazed not only at the civil discourse that the students had clearly practiced but also by the level of academic and content language that they used to wrangle through the exercise. It was clear from the way the teacher presented the material and the way the students engaged with it that this Joint Productive Activity was not an isolated event. It had come not only after weeks of practicing *how* to converse intentionally and purposefully, but also following several lessons introducing the topic of the Holocaust and discussing and analyzing the novel, giving the students enough background knowledge (through shared classroom context) to connect to and support their reasoning.

**JPA Task Card: The Impact of the Teacher
in Independent-JPAs vs. IC-JPAs, continued**

As we walked around the room, observing the Independent-JPAs, we could see the strength of the activity in sponsoring rich and deep conversation. Students were discussing not only the more prosaic descriptive details of the photos but were also making deep inferences such as, "[The children in the concentration camp] are all wearing the same thing like they don't have individual identities, but the others [in the Japanese internment camp] have their own clothes and look like they are still individuals." Or, "The Japanese children look like they have more freedom because they have more space."

The teacher had selected a group of students, who were not quite ready to participate in this activity as an Independent-JPA, to participate with her in an IC-JPA instead. She was present throughout the lesson to formatively assess who was still shaky on the concepts and to ask probing questions, such as, "Tell me more about what you notice about the fences?" She also invited more reticent students into the conversation: "Sara said she noticed that the children in the concentration camps look colder; do you agree, Quatravius?" Her presence bumped up the lesson and focused the learning so her instructional goal was met, while providing a safe, scaffolded environment for the students to practice collaborative conversation. The JPA was simple (identify similarities and differences using descriptive adjectives in a T-Chart), but the conversation was deep and rich and went well beyond recall. The pace of the lesson was measured, not rushed, and all the students were attentive and participating, if not at the same levels.

- With your PLC, grade-level team or other group, consider the student and teacher interactions in each type of JPA.
- Identify on sticky notes indicators of the foundational Safe Environment, student and teacher Habits of Collaboration, Deep Listening, and Complex Questioning evident in the Independent-JPAs and IC-JPA described.
- As you discuss each of the elements, decide whether the comments on your sticky notes reflect on and discuss the advantages of Independent-JPAs vs. IC-JPAs as evidenced in the text.

**JPA TASK CARD: THE IMPACT OF THE TEACHER
IN INDEPENDENT-JPAS VS. IC-JPAS, CONTINUED**

Questions to Consider

- What makes an effective IC-JPA?
- How can the teacher be at the table to facilitate and deepen the complexity of the learning without shutting the conversation down?
- What are the dangers of teachers taking too much control of the conversation? What are the dangers of their absence or silence?
- Looking at the Venn diagram your group created, when might you choose to utilize an Independent-JPA? An IC-JPA? What about the students, classroom, content, and instructional goal might influence your decision?

Additionally, IC-JPAs provide a chance for the teacher to be the learner. As we discussed previously, students come to the classroom with a lifetime of lived experience, and as teachers allow space for students to make meaningful connections to what they are teaching (and as teachers listen to these connections), they are offered the chance to learn new ways of thinking as well as new concepts and applications. Finally, IC-JPAs allow teachers a more intimate moment with intentionally grouped students to celebrate student successes. Essentially, what makes an IC-JPA special is that it enriches the lesson by truly joining the teacher and student sides of the Arch. Table 6.1 summarizes the benefits of both kinds of JPAs.

At the same time, first attempts at implementing IC-JPAs can present their own set of pitfalls. It can be difficult for teachers to relinquish control and allow for a shift in the way teachers and students interact (Gokee, 2017). IC-JPAs are student-centered rather than teacher-centered, representing a paradigm shift; it can take time, reflection, and practice to learn new habits of collaboration. This can be challenging because while the role of the teacher in an IC-JPA is not to control the lesson, neither is it to be a passive observer. *The teacher's presence as an engaged facilitator matters.* The power of teachers' contributions to the learning that takes place in an IC-JPA cannot be overstated.

However, whether you are running IC-JPAs or Independent-JPAs (or both), remember that your role as teacher is *fundamental* before, during, and after the lesson implementation (Gokee, 2017). It is vital to bring the group back at the end and close the lesson with a group debrief, underscoring the instructional goals, clearing up misconceptions, and lifting student understanding to a higher level.

Table 6.1. Benefits of Independent-JPAs vs. IC-JPAs

Benefits	Independent-JPA	IC-JPA
Instructional	Provides students with opportunities to: • build autonomy • practice tasks that are familiar but within their ZPD • connect concepts • scaffold for one another • hear and understand multiple perspectives • participate in low stakes environment to practice new processes Provides teacher with opportunities to: • conduct an IC-JPA (because the rest of the students are autonomously engaged in other tasks) • integrate collaborative, conversation-based instruction within school's curricular initiatives	Provides students with opportunities to: • build autonomy • scaffold for one another • hear and understand multiple perspectives • participate in low-stakes environment to practice new processes Provides teacher with opportunities to: • model language and offer corrective feedback • push students through ZPD • address students' misconceptions • reteach • provide enrichment • dig deeper • integrate collaborative, conversation-based instruction within school's curricular initiatives • structure intentional grouping according to interests, learning styles, abilities, personality dynamics, etc.
Community Building	• Builds SEL • Provides an opportunity to develop leadership • Provides a space for the quiet/introverted to engage in and share ideas	• Builds SEL • Provides an opportunity to develop leadership • Provides a space for the quiet/introverted to engage in and share ideas
Assessment	Provides limited space for: • Formative assessment *(How are they doing?)* • Informal assessment before a unit test *(What do I need to reteach?)* • Formal assessment *(Have we met the standard?)*	Provides space for focused and targeted: • Formative assessment *(How are they doing?)* • Informal assessment before a unit test *(What do I need to reteach?)* • Formal assessment *(Have we met the standard?)*

BUILDING A JOINT PRODUCTIVE ACTIVITY (JPA)

So how do teachers create Joint Productive Activities that will engage students, but not represent so much work or something so different from what they already do that they will never want to do them? The initial planning is the same for implementing Independent-JPA or IC-JPAs. Despite teachers' experience creating collaborative lessons or asking deep questions that provoke conversation, it can be a daunting task to create lessons that integrate all the building blocks of the Arch—ensuring that the lessons provide rigorous content and language goals, that they are contextualized for relevance, and that they are framed within a structure that requires collaboration and conversation.

To facilitate this planning process, we have created a tool (a menu of sorts) to help guide teachers in the planning process. We'd like to think of this as "building a JPA burrito." To start, imagine you are at one of those restaurants where they have the menu that asks you to (1) select the wrap or container you would like to have your meal in (taco, burrito, bowl, salad, etc.); (2) pick your protein; (3) choose the veggie toppings you want to enhance the meal; and (4) pick the salsa or condiments you want to spice it up. A burrito has the perfect combination of nutritional elements (protein, veggies, and salsa!) all held together in a single structure. If we think of the burrito as a metaphor for the JPA, we can break down the lesson-planning process into four parts, where each of the parts corresponds to the stages of building your perfect burrito. In this extended metaphor, the "wrap/container" represents the JPA structure/process; the "protein" represents the content goals; the "veggies" are the language goals; and the "topping/salsa" is how we contextualize the lesson to make it relevant. When combined together they create the perfect tasty meal—sorry, lesson.

Step 1: Choose your Wrap/Container: JPA Structure

Look at the Build Your Own JPA Burrito chart (Table 6.2). The first step to planning a JPA is to *choose a structure*. This is the lesson's "wrap" or "container"; it defines the form that the product will take. Just as the soft flour tortilla or bowl or hard corn tortilla is for the burrito, the JPA structure is the container for the final lesson product. Will your JPA task ask your students to collectively complete a sorting or matching exercise? Create a T-Chart? Design a thought map? Fill out a cloze exercise? Plot a graph? The structure will depend on what your goals are (see Table 6.3, Types of JPA Structures). There are a variety of JPA styles to choose from, and we suggest that you choose a structure based on the following criteria: (1) your *instructional goal* (Ask yourself: Does this particular type of activity help students meet this particular instructional goal? For example, if the instructional goal is to have students practice comparing and contrasting, a Venn diagram or a "Which One Doesn't Belong" structure might serve better than a T-Chart or a Sequence); (2) *the students' needs and experience* (Ask yourself: Is this a process that they have practiced? Do they need to be exposed to a new structure? Can they do this independently or will they need your support? How might that impact the level of content you teach in this lesson?); and (at least initially) (3) *what works best for you?* (Ask yourself: What structure am I most comfortable with? Remember that this is a learning process for you as well as for your students; you will be able to support them best if you feel confident with the structures that you ask them to use. Once you and your students are more familiar with the JPA process in general you can begin branching out to new structures.)

Learning to eat food wrapped in a tortilla shell takes practice, and so does learning JPA processes. Therefore, it is important that students know how to do these processes and have practice doing them before you fill in the structure with layered or complex content. For example, you can begin by teaching them one or two JPA structures (e.g., a Sort or a T-Chart), using content that is familiar, engaging, and not cognitively challenging. Once students know how to do a sorting exercise, you can create sorting JPAs again and again, layering in new and more complex content. In this way, even when the level of challenge and complexity of the content increases, the students will know how to approach the exercise and feel confident in attacking it independently because the *process is familiar* and the structure of the exercise is known. Table 6.3 outlines some different JPA structure examples you might consider as you plan, including what kinds of instructional goals each might support, their advantages/disadvantages, and how each one works. This list is by no means exhaustive and is meant only to give an idea of what is possible. We encourage you to use this chart to plan JPAs, reflecting on the advantages and disadvantages of each as you consider which structure type will best facilitate your instructional goals. We would like to underscore the importance of aligning the task structure with your instructional goals. This ensures that the JPA product will actually work as a tool to solidify the students' understanding of the content. Furthermore, having a product that the students have to collaboratively produce supports CLD learners and builds literacy by attaching the words and ideas from the discussion to visible, physical artifacts that students can manipulate, create, and use as a base for follow-up activities.

Table 6.2. Building Your Own JPA Burrito

	1. What "Wrap/Container" would you like?	2. What "Protein" would you like?	3. What "Veggies" would you like?	4. What "Topping/Salsa" would you like?
What does this component do?	*This is the structure of the product (or type of problem) that holds the activity together, just as a tortilla or bowl is the "container" for a burrito.*	*This is the complex, standards-based content that you want the students to learn through this lesson. It's the "meat" of the lesson.*	*This is the language concept or metalinguistic skill/process that you want the students to practice. Like the peppers, onions, tomatoes, or cilantro that you add to a burrito, this gives the protein texture and flavor.*	*This is the context that makes the learning relevant and real. Like the salsa, guacamole, or sour cream, it blends into the other components and binds them together so they will "stick."*
Questions to ask as you build your lesson	• What is the best structure to meet my instructional goals? • What is the best structure to provide a deeper understanding of this content? • What are the students producing? • Does this structure require collaboration? • Is it complex enough to promote rich conversation?	• What is/are the content standard(s) I would like them to learn with this lesson? • What complex questions can I ask to deepen conceptual understanding? • Are there multiple complementary, cross-disciplinary standards that can work together?	• What language concepts/skills or metalinguistic processes would I like the students to practice? • How does this language goal support the content goal? • What specific ELA or Speaking and Listening Standards might be practiced here?	• What previous lessons can I connect to this lesson? • What background knowledge does this group of students have that can be intentionally activated with this lesson? • What visual, auditory, or tactile representations can I include in the lesson to connect this to things my students know?

1. What "Wrap/Container" would you like?	2. What "Protein" would you like?	3. What "Veggies" would you like?	4. What "Topping/Salsa" would you like?
Examples of Possible Types/ Options	• Sort • "Stick It" • Graph • "Eliminate It" • Mosaic • Dichotomous Key • Puzzle • Sequence • Chart • Venn Diagram • Timeline • Cloze Passage • "Which One Doesn't Belong"	Content standards: • Math • Science • Social Studies • ELA, etc.	• Genre Re-write • Roots/Affixes • L1/L2 Comparison • Inference • Paraphrasing • De-coding • Sentence structure • Word creation • Word categories • Verb agreement • Vocabulary
			• Pictures/diagrams/graphs/ graphics • Realia/manipulatives • Verbal and written references to previous lessons • Songs or sound recordings

Table 6.3. Types of JPA Structures

Type of JPA (what kind of PRODUCT?)	When would this be appropriate? What types of instructional goals would this support?	What are the advantages/ disadvantages?	How does it work?
Sort	This is appropriate for instructional goals that require classifying, categorizing, or distinguishing between or among different components.	Sorting structures can be beneficial as you are first introducing the process of JPAs. However, a disadvantage is that there is usually one clear answer. Nonetheless, as students become more familiar with JPAs it can be advantageous to have more ambiguous or multiple answers (i.e., one item can be sorted into multiple categories) that will cause students to examine their thinking and support their answers.	The students are usually given individual strips or cards with key words, concepts, images, or phrases and asked to work together to sort them (e.g., a set of sentences/ phrases that are to be classified into fragments, run-ons, simple sentences, complex sentences, or compound sentences).
Chart	Charts are appropriate for instructional goals that require students to visually organize disparate pieces of information and show the relationships among parts.	Charts help students visually separate information and serve as a graphic organizer; can easily be done as a group with one product at the end; and can be used across subjects and with a variety of different thinking process goals.	The chart type chosen depends on the kind of data and the goal of the lesson, but a few common ones are T-charts, four-square charts, graphs, diagrams, and flowcharts.

Venn Diagram	Venn diagrams are appropriate for instructional goals that support identifying attributes of two or more ideas, items, people, etc. and comparing and contrasting them.	Venn diagrams can help students organize information visually and allow students to see the relationships between key ideas, items, people, etc.	Students are usually asked to compare/contrast two (or more) ideas, items, people, etc., and to explore the similarities and differences between them, placing the similarities in the middle overlapping space of the Venn diagram. (Venn diagrams are usually created on large chart paper so that there is one for the group and everyone can work together, rather than individual ones.)
Sequence/ Order	Creating a sequence or order is appropriate for instructional goals that require students to understand the order or sequence of something.	Ordering may help students see the bigger picture and be able to relate events to others; understand the steps in a process; understand cause and effect; and understand storyline. A disadvantage is that there is usually one clear answer.	Students are given individual strips or cards with key words, concepts, images, or phrases and asked to work together to place them in the correct order.
Timeline	A timeline is appropriate for instructional goals that have a time element incorporated where understanding how/when events occur in relation to others is important.	Making timelines may help students see the bigger picture and be able to relate events to others, understand historical events, understand a character's life, or understand a process; could be used as a writing brainstorm tool; and could be used across subjects. A disadvantage is that there may be one clear answer.	In this activity, students create a graphical representation of the given prompt by placing items, actions, events, etc. sequentially along a line organized by a specified span of time (of day, of an event, of a year, of a life, etc.). Students may place already written cards or write or draw their own representation.

Table 6.3. Types of JPA Structures, continued

Mosaic	A mosaic is appropriate for instructional goals that require students to take disparate ideas and create a new product that synthesizes the ideas.	This structure's advantages include that it requires students to use higher order thinking skills such as synthesizing information and creating something new; allows students to be creative, as there is not one right answer or way to create the product; and can be used across subjects.	In this type of activity, students take pieces from separate sources and as a group combine them into a single product (e.g., students each bring a line of a poem and as a group create a new poem using each individual's phrases; or each student thinks of one important piece of advice that would have helped a character in a story and the students create a "top three pieces of advice" list for that character).
Stick It	This is appropriate for instructional goals that require students to come to a consensus on one "best" answer to a prompt as a group.	This structure can be used across disciplines (e.g., a math problem, question, or a question about the main idea of a story the class is reading); gives individual think time to engage each student in the process; and requires students to defend their thinking and communicate with each other to decide on a group answer.	The group is given a problem, question, prompt, etc. Each student gets a sticky note to come up with their own answer before coming together to discuss their individual thoughts and decide on one best answer as a group with everyone's input.
Eliminate It	This is appropriate for instructional goals that require classifying, categorizing or distinguishing between or among different components.	This structure's advantages include encouraging students to communicate and defend their answer because there could be more than one "right" answer; can be used to have students explore components of new material OR with review material that students should know; can be used across subjects; and can have multiple correct answers as the answer depends on the evidence the group comes up with to support it.	Students discuss and decide which of four items (or pictures) should be excluded from a group, and defend their answers. For example, there could be 4 representations of numbers and a student may eliminate one because the other 3 are all the same representation (e.g., an array) or may eliminate the number 3 because the other pictures all represent the number 7 (but in different ways). Elimination could also be used in classification in science where items could be eliminated for different attributes, depending on what students argue for (similar to "Which one doesn't belong?").

Step 2: Pick your Protein: Content Instructional Goals

Once you have decided on your JPA burrito style, then you can decide what "protein" or content objectives, you want to fill your JPA burrito with. This is the "meat" of the lesson, what we really want the students to learn and what is going to "feed" them. Just as when you create a tasty burrito you can have primary and complementary proteins (chicken as well as rice and beans) you can have a primary content objective (your main instructional goal) as well as complementary content objectives that support and give contextual references to your primary objectives. It is important to remember that these content goals can be interdisciplinary. For example, math content objectives can be enriched if they are integrated with science content objectives and social studies content objectives can benefit from being embedded in ELA units. Imagine you are designing a math JPA and your primary content objective is to have students practice the concept of percentages. Rather than having the students work on decontextualized problems, you might consider embedding percentage problems in a social studies context. In this way, the students get practice with math percentages (primary content objective), while reinforcing what they know and are learning in social studies (secondary content objective). And because these concepts are applied to real world examples, the concepts are both more engaging and more readily understood.

Step 3: Choose your Veggies: Language Goals

Once you have determined what your "protein" is, you must decide what "veggies" you want. The "veggies" are the language goals. These are the not the "meat" of the JPA burrito, but give the burrito texture and color while providing vital nutrients. Teachers may inadvertently neglect language goals when focusing on other content goals, but remember that just as protein and veggies are both necessary for a healthy diet, content and language work together supporting one another, and both need our focus. Without language, our students cannot access, manipulate, or thoroughly comprehend concepts. Therefore, it is vital to consider what language students need in order to understand specific concepts (see Chapter 5 on integrating language and literacy goals into lessons). Finally, recall that all content areas have their own "languages": styles, specific vocabularies, genres, and argument structures that must be consciously taught. Therefore, teachers must be intentional about choosing language goals and integrating them to support content goals across the curricula. We have developed a list of examples to consider (see Table 6.2). But remember, language goals should be chosen to complement and support content goals, not to stand alone or to fight with them.

NOTES FROM THE FIELD:
INTEGRATING MULTIPLE CONTENT AREAS INTO A SINGLE JPA

Reflect on the following vignette and questions to consider.

A 5th-grade class had been studying Westward Expansion and the role of the railroad in connecting the East with the West, and the teacher wanted to integrate a math lesson into the social studies context to enrich the learning for both subjects. She had designed a lesson where the students began activating their background knowledge by discussing the relative risks and benefits of selling cattle in the West or shipping them to the East. The students knew that they could make $20/head of cattle if they sold their cows in the West, but could make $100/head if they shipped them and sold them in the East.

The JPA had three steps and asked the students: (1) to calculate how much money they could make on 100 head of cattle sold in the West compared to 100 head sold in the East; (2) to determine the margin of profit they might lose if they knew that they would lose 20 to 25% of the cattle in the transport from West to East due to illness or cattle rustling, etc.; and (3) to reflect on what they learned in steps 1 and 2 and write a paragraph proposing a plan for selling their 100 head of cattle that would maximize profit while minimizing risk.

The students had a rich and productive discussion connecting what could have been decontextualized math to real and relevant problem-solving and integrated content.

Questions to Consider

- How can JPAs help us multiply our teaching time by folding multiple learning objectives into one lesson?
- How can JPAs provide authentic opportunities for our students to apply and transfer their knowledge?

Step 4: Choose your Toppings/Salsa to Spice it Up: Contextualization

Finally, the last thing we add to our burrito is the "topping/salsa" to "spice it up." The salsa you choose will add spice and zest and will serve to bind the other flavors and textures together. This is the *contextualization* of your JPA. How teachers contextualize lessons will vary depending on their students—what works for one student might not work for another. Remember the type of sauce that one person likes, that will make the food taste good to them, depends on their background, what they are used to, and what they need. The same is true in contextualizing for students. Context matters:

JPA Task Card: Deconstructing a 7th Grade JPA

Instructional Goals

- To analyze the structure and content of a JPA
- To become familiar with the JPA-Burrito Chart as well as the JPA Structure Chart

Task Activities

In your PLC:

- Reference Table 6.2, Building Your Own JPA Burrito.
- Divide a piece of chart paper into four blocks to create a 4-square chart.
  - » Wrap/Container (JPA Structure/product)
  - » Protein/Meat (Content Goals)
  - » Veggies (Language Goals)
  - » Topping (Contextualization)
- Read the Task Card, "Student JPA Task Card: *Matching Galapagos Tortoises to their Islands*" for 7th-grade Science students engaged in an Independent-JPA.
- Complete the 4-square chart, identifying the lesson's structure, content goals, language goals, and how the teacher contextualized the lesson for the students.
- Give evidence to support your reasoning.

Questions to Consider

- How do language goals complement content instructional goals?
- How does the structure of the task support the content and language goals?
- How would you adapt this Task Card differentiating for different student needs?

Knowing where students are from, what they know, and what is relevant for them will determine how teachers contextualize and make the JPA real and applicable.

When putting together a JPA, bear in mind that none of these parts would make a good meal on its own. Doing a sorting task separate from any instructional goals would be like eating a bare tortilla, and if all a teacher focused on were contextualization without any content to rest it on, it would be like eating salsa straight from the jar. Salsa must have something to flavor, just as context needs content to give it meaning.

STUDENT JPA TASK CARD: MATCHING GALAPAGOS TORTOISES TO THEIR ISLANDS

Contextualizing the Lesson

The Galapagos Islands are an archipelago of volcanic islands off the coast of Ecuador, a country in Northeastern South America. The islands are known for their vast number of endemic species and were studied by Charles Darwin, who used his observations from these islands to develop his theory of evolution.

The species we will be focusing on today is the Galapagos tortoise and the varieties that inhabit three of the islands in the archipelago: Pinta Island, Isabela Island, and Hood Island. The tortoises living on each island have evolved so they can survive in the specific conditions on that island.

Use the resources provided to complete the task. Good luck and HAVE FUN!

Side note: the word *Galapagos* comes from an old Spanish word meaning tortoise—how cool is that?

Instructional Goal(s)

CONTENT

7th-grade Science standard—Students will examine the evolution of living organisms through inherited characteristics that promote survival of organisms and the survival of successive generations of their offspring.

- I can explain what physical characteristics of organisms have changed over successive generations and speculate as to why.
- I can describe ways in which species on Earth evolved due to natural selection.

LANGUAGE

- I can annotate texts, identifying evidence to support a claim.
- I can make a claim and support it with textual evidence.
- I can discuss evidence to solve a problem and come to consensus with my peers.
- I can write a summary.

Unwrapping the JPA Burrito

Now that you have had a chance to think about how to plan a JPA, let's take a look at a JPA lesson and try to break it down. The following two exercises are designed to give you the opportunity to play with the JPA burrito components and think about how they work together by analyzing a JPA lesson. Broadly, these activities are both based on the same 7th-grade science

**STUDENT JPA TASK CARD: MATCHING GALAPAGOS TORTOISES
TO THEIR ISLANDS, CONTINUED**

JPA Task Structure: Matching (with answers recorded on Answer Template provided below)

Task Materials

- Pictures (in plastic sleeves) of three Galapagos tortoises in their environments
- Maps and descriptions (in plastic sleeves) of three Galapagos islands where these tortoises live
- Expo Markers
- Answer template

Task Activities

- Go over conversational norms.
- Each member of the group chooses and shares their conversational goal.
- Examine the pictures of the tortoises and the descriptions of each island provided.
- Annotate the pictures and maps with the Expo marker—identifying factors that provide evidence linking the tortoises to the islands.
- Match each tortoise (1, 2, or 3) to its corresponding island.
- On the template provided below, record your group's rationale for your decisions.
- Provide evidence from the pictures to support your claim.
- Remember to:
  » Focus on the characteristics of the TORTOISE (the neck, limbs, shell, etc.), not the environment
  » READ THE ENTIRE DESCRIPTION OF THE ISLAND, not just part!

Questions to Consider

- How do animals adapt to their environment?
- What kinds of things cause adaptations to occur?
- Based on your scientific observations of the pictures and evidence from the island descriptions, what kinds of adaptations did the tortoises make? What factors provoked these adaptations?

**STUDENT JPA TASK CARD: MATCHING GALAPAGOS TORTOISES
TO THEIR ISLANDS, CONTINUED**

Debrief/Lesson Reflection

Content

- What impacts might global warming (i.e., increasing temperatures, more frequent droughts, rising sea levels, etc.) have on the Galapagos tortoises? How might they adapt?
- How might we ameliorate these impacts?

Process

- What strategies did your group use to arrive at a conclusion?
- Was every group member's thinking taken into consideration?

Follow-Up Activity

Write a report imagining changes in a given species' environment (i.e., availability of preferred food or water, changes in temperature or rainfall, alterations in habitat, etc.) speculating on how this species might adapt to survive these changes.

Galapagos Islands/Tortoise Matching JPA—Answer Template

Record your group's rationale for which tortoise matches which island. Provide specific evidence to support your decisions.

   Our group thinks Tortoise (1, 2, or 3) _____ matches_____ island, because:

   Our group thinks Tortoise (1, 2, or 3) _____ matches_____ island, because:

   Our group thinks Tortoise (1, 2, or 3) _____ matches_____ island, because:

Summarize your group's thoughts about how/why the tortoises adapted here:

JPA Task Card: Analyzing a 7th-grade JPA Lesson

Instructional Goal

To analyze a JPA lesson and identify evidence of the Arch system.

Task Activities

- Review the Arch diagram, Figure 1.1.
- Read the Scenario *"Observation of a 7th-Grade Science JPA—What's Going On?"* as well as the Task Card "Student JPA Task Card: *Matching Galapagos Tortoises to their Islands"* you used in the previous activity.
- While reading, think about all we have discussed about how the Arch components work together as a system (*i.e., the columns, the scaffolding, the keystone, etc.*).
- Write down specific examples from the text that illustrate the components of the Arch.
- As a group discuss what you noticed and using the 4-column chart provided on the next page, write evidence from the scenario provided below, write evidence from the scenario for the student side in column two and for the teacher side in column four. *Note: evidence might fit with more than one component.*

Questions to Consider

- What components of the Arch did you identify? What was your evidence?
- What components were you not able to identify?
- Can you remember anything else that represents the "missing areas" on your Arch?

---

lesson and materials. The first JPA (see JPA Task Card: Deconstructing a 7th Grade JPA) asks you to examine the task card and materials provided and to deconstruct the JPA lesson, identifying: (1) the wrap, the JPA structure that holds the lesson together (what product the students are being asked to collaboratively produce); (2) the protein, the content instructional goals that are the main instructional focus; (3) the veggies, the language goals that support those instructional goals; and (4) the salsa, how the teacher contextualized the lesson. The second JPA (see JPA Task Card: Analyzing a 7th Grade JPA Lesson) asks that you read the narrative description of the JPA activity and analyze it—identifying how the Arch system is evident in the enactment of the lesson.

JPA Task Card 2: Analyzing a 7th-grade JPA Lesson, continued

OBSERVATION OF A 7TH-GRADE SCIENCE JPA—WHAT'S GOING ON?

The day we came to visit this 7th-grade science class, the students were engaged in a JPA sorting activity about tortoises in the Galapagos Islands. They had been studying the theory and principles of evolution (7th-grade Science standard S7L5), discussing the ideas and concepts as well as the vocabulary for a week before this JPA. The students were familiar with Darwin's study of the Galapagos, and how he had noticed that differences in the islands' geography and vegetation had impacted the evolution of the different animals there. Ms. Huddleston activated some of this background knowledge before the students began the JPA by referencing the lesson from the previous class.

When we arrived to observe the lesson, the class, which was a general education, mixed-ability group, was busily participating in the activity. The students, who were uniformly engaged and animatedly discussing the photos and maps at their tables, were arranged in six clusters of four or five students working around a folder with a single task card and one set of shared materials. Ms. Huddleston informed us that the class was used to working independently in small groups and that she changed them every few weeks so that the students would become used to working with different people. These groups had been carefully chosen according to both who worked well together and by ability (i.e., sorted into low-middle and middle-high ability regarding access to content understanding and science writing ability). However, the groups were heterogeneously mixed by gender as well as language ability (ELs were distributed across groups). Each group was given the same set of materials (maps of the different Galapagos islands, texts with descriptions of the islands, and pictures of tortoises). However, some groups had been given pictures with annotations on them (focusing the students' attention on the tortoises' physical features that the students should take into account as they worked together). All the students were collaborating on the same activity: to analyze the physical features of the tortoises, read the information about the physical characteristics of the islands, and determine which tortoise belonged to which island.

We noticed that there were several numbered sets of classroom norms posted on the wall and asked Ms. Huddleston about them. "Oh, yeah, we developed norms with each group. This is group 3. Their norms are over there." Pointing, she indicated a sheet on the inside wall, above a row of cabinets. "We go over them every time we have small groups when we choose our conversation goals for the day. You came in right after we finished today."

JPA Task Card 2: Analyzing a 7th-grade JPA Lesson, continued

As Ms. Huddleston made circuits around the room, checking in with each table multiple times to see where they might be stalled or have misconceptions, we observed and listened to the students' interactions. The group nearest the door had the annotated tortoises. The tallest of the four, a vivacious girl with a mass of tight, dark curls who stood with one leg propped on her chair, leaned across the pictures with her elbows resting on the table. The card in front of her indicated that her goal was to invite others to share their ideas. She gazed intently at the photos of the tortoises. "See?" she said, pointing to the space in the shell on tortoise #3, "It says there is lots of room to move, but this one," indicating tortoise #1, "doesn't."

"What does that mean?" asked the quiet, petite brunette sitting next to her. "Why would that matter?"

"I'm not sure," said the first girl, "What do you think, Saiya?" looking at a third girl at the table whose goal card stated that she was working on contributing more. Saiya shifted in her chair and pulled the picture of tortoise #3 as well as the map and description of Island A toward her. She read the text under her breath, stumbling on a couple of the words: "Gr-grazing on the island has di-diminished due to an exotic species of feral? feeral? goat . . ." she stopped reading and looked up, "What's feral?"

"Maybe wild?" responded the brunette. "We have feral cats living in the woods behind our neighborhood that are always coming out and knocking over the trash cans."

"Hmm," Saiya muttered, continuing to ponder over the papers. "I think," she began after a moment, "that maybe it means that the turtles have changed because they needed to reach their food." She paused and pulling the picture of tortoise #1 next to tortoise #3, continued, "I mean, look. This one can't move its head at all, it would be hard for it to grab anything really high. It's like when Shawana wore that jacket that was too small for her and she couldn't lift her arms!" The table dissolved into laughter and Shawana, the tall girl, cocked her head to one side and clicking her tongue, retorted, "I like that jacket!"

"But still," continued Saiya, "you couldn't reach your books in your locker. Jamal had to help you pull them down. It's like that with the turtle." At that moment, Ms. Huddleston moved to the table to see what the laughter was about. "What are you thinking?" she asked the group.

Again, Saiya pointed at tortoise #1. "Look, it can't move its head high so no way it's gonna be able to get food up on trees. It's gonna need stuff low on the ground or it will starve." The rest of the group looked at the pictures. Shawana turned the picture of tortoise #1 toward her and moved it next to the description of Island B.

JPA Task Card 2: Analyzing a 7th-grade JPA Lesson, continued

"I'm glad that you are working on your goals!" Ms. Huddleston asserted, nodding particularly at Saiya, who rarely spoke up, and Shawana, for whom it was a challenge to not dominate the conversation. She touched the pictures Shawana had paired and asked, "Okay, so I hear you say that this tortoise can't move its head much so it can't reach the vegetation that is high, but what do you think that means about how it has evolved because of its environment? What kind of vegetation would it need? Which island do you think this tortoise lives on?"

"Oh!" exclaimed Shawana. "It's Island B! Look! It says it has diverse vegetation."

"Do you all agree?" Ms. Huddleston asked. The girls looked at each other and then back at the maps and pictures. "Why would that matter?" Ms. Huddleston prodded, "What evidence do you have to support your reasoning? Discuss how you are going to write your argument for tortoise #1 being on Island B." With that she walked to the next group.

After 20 minutes or so, the groups were winding down and finishing up their product, pairing the tortoises to the islands and offering a collective written response with evidence for their choices. Ms. Huddleston came to the front of the room and called their attention, asking them what they had determined and why. She then did a masterful job of debriefing what the students had discussed. Using pictures on the smartboard and gestures for illustration, she reinforced the main points she had wanted them to learn (as part of her instructional goal), and modeled the academic vocabulary in the now familiar context. Finally, she asked the students to review their conversation goals and to rate themselves and their group, recording their rating on their cards.

Layering Content into the Process

As part of the purposeful planning process, the balance between content and process is something that must be continually gauged. Students are not often familiar with the processes necessary for collaborative conversations, and getting them sufficiently accustomed to them so that they can be autonomous can take time and requires practice. Teachers must consider this as they plan lessons. Asking students to integrate too much new or complex content at the same time as they engage in a new process can limit their success. Therefore, it is vital that students be given enough time to learn the process with less cognitively challenging content; then as they become more familiar with the process, the teacher can increase the complexity of the content (Grube, Ryan, Lowell, & Stringer, 2018; Wong, Wong, & Seroyer,

JPA Task Card 2: Analyzing a 7th-grade JPA Lesson, continued

FOUR-COLUMN CHART—
EVIDENCE OF ARCH COMPONENTS IN CLASSROOM SCENARIO (cont.)

Student Side of Arch	Evidence from Scenario	Teacher Side of Arch	Evidence from Scenario
Foundation: Safe Classroom Environment		Foundation: Safe Classroom Environment	
Scaffolding: Student Listening		Scaffolding: Teacher Listening	
Scaffolding: Student Purposeful Planning		Scaffolding: Teacher Purposeful Planning	
Scaffolding: Complex Questions		Scaffolding: Complex Questions	
Scaffolding: Task Card		Scaffolding: Task Card	
Scaffolding: Habits of Collaboration		Scaffolding: Habits of Collaboration	
Columns/Assets: Student Home Language		Columns/Assets: Teacher Home Language	
Columns/Assets: Student Background Knowledge		Columns/Assets: Teacher Background Knowledge	
Columns/Assets: Student Social Interaction Skills		Columns/Assets: Teacher Social Interaction Skills	
Columns/Assets: Student Content Literacy Skills		Columns/Assets: Teacher Content Literacy Skills	
Columns/Assets: Student Motivation		Columns/Assets: Teacher Motivation	

JPA TASK CARD 2: ANALYZING A 7TH-GRADE JPA LESSON, CONTINUED

FOUR-COLUMN CHART—
EVIDENCE OF ARCH COMPONENTS IN CLASSROOM SCENARIO (CONT.)

Columns/Assets: Student Aptitudes	Columns/Assets: Teacher Aptitudes
Voussoirs: Practicing Language and Literacy	Voussoirs: Focusing on Language and Literacy
Voussoirs: Making Meaningful Connections	Voussoirs: Contex- tualizing Lessons for Meaning
Voussoirs: Engaging in Challenging and Complex Activities	Voussoirs: Design- ing Challenging and Complex Activities
Voussoirs: Working in Collaboration with others	Voussoirs: Creating Opportunities for Collaboration
Voussoirs: Learning through Purposeful Conversation	Voussoirs: Teaching through Purposeful Conversation
Keystone: Joint Productive Activity	Keystone: Joint Productive Activity

---

2005). This can take time; however, the benefits of creating automaticity in the process are enormous.

Do not let the time necessary to familiarize students with these JPA processes (and the habits of collaboration) daunt you or dissuade you from persisting in establishing a system of collaborative, conversation-based instruction in your classroom. As one of our teachers says, "You start out slow, so you can go fast!" Once you have the routines established, the investment of time pays great dividends. You will spend less time giving instructions and disciplining because your students will know what to do. Additionally, you multiply your teaching time and can be more strategic in your instruction because you will have a clearer idea of where your students need (and don't need) support. The beauty and strength of JPAs is that they

---

**NOTES FROM THE FIELD: PLANNING INTERDISCIPLINARY LESSONS
TO DEEPEN UNDERSTANDING**

One of our 5th-grade teachers was teaching a science unit with the standard
to identify the differences between human-made and natural disasters. To
promote deep thinking about this topic, she crafted a JPA lesson that an-
chored the analysis of human-made and natural disasters in a discussion
about the drought and arson-provoked fire in the novel *Esperanza Rising* that
they had been reading in ELA. By teaching these in an integrated way, she
created spaces for the students to connect their new learning to a context
they were already familiar with and to apply it in a real and authentic way.

Question to Consider

- How would teaching layered lessons integrating interdisciplinary
  subjects help our students to learn and apply new knowledge?

---

allow students to engage more deeply with the content than they would
normally have the opportunity to do.

As teachers, we are under constant pressure to cover more material, in
less time, for an increasingly diverse student population. With all the challenges, it becomes clear that if we were to line up all the content standards
in a linear fashion, we would never be able to teach all of them. It therefore
is in our best interest, and that of our students, to be teaching multiple
standards that support one another at the *same time*. But herein lies the rub:
how does one teach multiple content standards in a single lesson (or series
of lessons) and ensure that a variety of integrated instructional goals are
met? The answer lies in purposeful, responsive planning and well-practiced
processes. A productive JPA integrates interrelated instructional goals that
support one another to promote student learning. Taking the content/pro-
cess balance into account (see Figure 6.2), teachers must be mindful of the
amount of content they are layering into any given lesson. In this sense, even
when we are trying to hit multiple content standards in one lesson, we must
guard against packing in too many instructional goals at once. Sometimes
teachers fear that if they don't ask a ream of questions, the students won't
have enough to talk about. But remember, the key to productive conversation isn't the number of questions or tasks, but the quality and complexity
of them.

In an effort to give students more of a challenge, teachers will often
just give students more problems or exercises to complete. While finishing more problems or reading more pages will certainly give students more
practice and perhaps increase fluency, it will do little to increase the level of

Figure 6.2. Process vs. Content

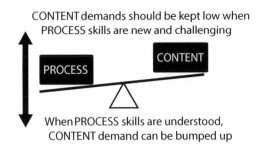

CONTENT demands should be kept low when
PROCESS skills are new and challenging

When PROCESS skills are understood,
CONTENT demand can be bumped up

FOOD FOR THOUGHT

Reflect on the thought below and Questions to Consider that follow.

"More is not equal to complex. Sometimes more is just . . . more."

Questions to Consider

- How is difficulty different from complexity?
- How do we sometimes confuse the two in our assignments?
- Why is it important for us to focus on complexity in our JPA tasks for students?

---

complexity that the students are able to tackle. We also fall into the trap of trying to make it more "complex" by including too many disparate goals into a single lesson. This can become confusing and overwhelming for the students. They may feel so much pressure to complete the task that they cannot pause to really consider the complexity of the question.

Remember, the goal is to go deeper, not wider. In the words of one 5th-grade student, "ICs are patient." If the process is established, and the lesson is contextualized (connected to content that the students are familiar with and related to real-life problems), then you can layer multiple content objectives because the students will know what to do. The key is to constantly reflect on the connections between instructional goals, the task, and the questions. Ask: How does this activity support this instructional goal? What questions are going to promote deeper and more complex thinking? How can we ensure that the activity will require collaboration among all group members?

JPA Task Card: Flipping a Lesson

Contextualizing the Lesson

Teachers are asked to build off the knowledge and understanding they gained from reading the book, as well as the work they have engaged in while teaching this school year.

Instructional Goal(s)

Content

- To practice working collaboratively to develop a Joint Productive Activity (JPA) Task Card from readily available resources.
- To practice incorporating the key elements of a Joint Productive Activity (JPA).

Language

- To reflect upon and practice the Habits of Collaboration tools utilized in the classroom.
- To consider how to incorporate language goals from all four domains (listening, speaking, reading, and writing) into our lessons.

Task Activities

- Working with a grade-level partner, review your conversational norms. Do you need to change or add any?
- Consider your conversational goal. Do you need to choose a new one? Share with your partner.
- Reflecting on your class, select a lesson that you think could easily be changed into a JPA (for example, a worksheet that you would normally assign to be completed individually).
- Using the Build your own JPA Burrito chart (see Table 6.2) and the Types of JPA Structures chart (see Table 6.3) as guides, choose for your JPA: a structure, an instructional goal, language goals, and how to contextualize *(think about your students as you decide)*.
- Using the Task Card template (presented in Chapter 4), work collaboratively to create a Teacher Task Card.
- Adapt your Teacher Task Card to create a Student Task Card. *You might use a QR code to record the task directions for CLD students.*
- Refer to Table 6.4, JPA Task Card Checklist, to make sure you have included all of the elements.
- Together, decide how to present your JPA task card lesson to the PLC for feedback.

JPA Task Card: Flipping a Lesson, continued

Questions to Consider

- How does the structure you have chosen (T-Chart, 4-Square, Venn diagram, etc.) support your instructional goal and promote student collaboration?
- How might you provide levels of differentiation to better support student autonomy?
- How did the Questions to Consider you chose for your JPA help to lift the students' thinking?
- How do your language goals support your discipline specific content goals?

Table 6.4. JPA Task Card Checklist

- Did you include ideas to **Contextualize** the activity for the students in your classroom?
- Did you include both a **Content Instructional Goal** *and* a **Language Instructional Goal**? (e.g., Speaking & Listening Standards, Academic Language, ELA Standards, Content Specific Language, etc.)
- Does your **JPA Task Structure** support your instructional goal?
- Are all of the **Task Materials** required to complete the activity included?
- Do your **Task Activities** require the students to *collaborate, discuss,* and *create a joint product*?
- Do your **Questions to Consider** enrich the JPA Activity, push the students into the "learning pit," or move students beyond surface learning to use complex thinking *during the task*?
- Did you include **Content Debrief/Reflection Questions** that ask your students to apply their learning in a new or different context *after they completed the task*?
- Did you include **Process Debrief/Reflection Questions** that ask your students to reflect on the process of the task and their participation in it *after they completed the task*?
- Did you include a **Follow-up Activity** (if appropriate)?

Figure 6.3. Sample Classroom Structure Configurations

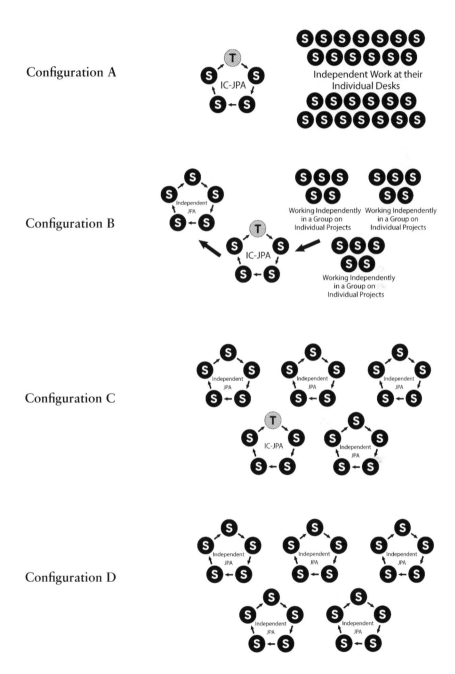

Finally, just as teachers must guard against giving students too many decontextualized or unrelated tasks, they must also guard against underestimating students. You know your students, and creating lessons that allow them to interact deeply and productively will help you to evaluate more clearly where their strengths and weaknesses are. But don't limit content because you think that they can't do it. Just make sure that they have enough to attach it to and have the tools to access it. *Our goal is to make the content more accessible, not less challenging.*

Planning Your Own JPA Lesson

Now that you have a clear idea of what a JPA looks like and how to plan a lesson, let's take what you know about your own class and lessons and apply it to the JPA format. The JPA Flipping a Lesson asks that you use the tools introduced in this chapter (Table 6.2, Building Your Own JPA Burrito; Table 6.3, Types of JPA Structures; and Table 6.4, JPA Task Card Checklist) as well as the Task Card Template discussed in Chapter 4 and available on the online webpage (coe.uga.edu/directory/latino-achievement) to modify a lesson that you already use, changing it into a JPA that would promote collaborative conversations.

CONSIDERATIONS FOR GETTING STARTED

As you begin to consider how to get started implementing the Arch system for collaborative, conversation-based instruction in your classroom, we encourage you to revisit the Arch. We recommend that you begin to develop a safe foundation by establishing speaking and listening norms with your students (see Chapter 2). Setting up the structures and habits needed to support the system while it is getting established may include helping your students to identify their conversation challenge, and then to set their goal for what they will focus on for improvement (see Chapter 4). The scaffolding is vital, and dedicating time to it is crucial to the successful implementation of JPAs. Once these elements are in place, you will need to think about how to create groups and organize your classroom so that you can implement JPAs. We suggest that you begin by selecting one group of students that you think is capable of handling the challenge of this new system and working with them until you all feel comfortable with the process. Remember that you are trying something new, just as your students are, so allow yourself some space for growing your new skill. Don't worry if the first time you try a JPA, it doesn't go as you had planned. Simply reflect on what happened (perhaps discuss it with your PLC and even with your students—they might be able to give you some insight!) and make appropriate changes, with the understanding that mastery is only achieved through practice.

Classroom Structure Examples

Another initial consideration is how to organize your classroom structures to begin integrating Independent-JPA and IC-JPA groups into your instructional blocks. In order for the teacher to be able to implement IC-JPAs, the other students in the classroom must be working autonomously, either individually or in groups. Only in this way will the teacher be able to focus his or her attention on the IC-JPA group without being distracted or called upon to support the other students. Ideally, we suggest that you move your students to engaged, collaborative group work, but you must begin with the structure that is most comfortable for you to begin fostering student autonomy in your classroom. Remember, this is a *process* and will take time to establish.

As we discussed in Chapter 4, one of the key organizational structures supporting the Arch system is the creation of centers, spaces for group-based instruction. If you already run centers that the students choose or rotate through, (e.g., one silent reading center, one computer center, one math center, etc.), as a first step, you may feel more comfortable running your usual centers and simply adding one IC-JPA center where you are present. Alternatively, you may run several small groups at the same time with all students doing the same JPA: Those groups who are ready can do that JPA as an Independent-JPA (working collaboratively in an independent group supporting each other), and the group that needs your attention the most (this might be the struggling students as well as those who need to have their learning accelerated) can do the JPA as an IC-JPA with you there to facilitate their group work. Another option is to create unit-based centers where, for example, you teach a mini-lesson about a topic in whole group with direct instruction and then your students must rotate through several different JPA centers (all Independent-JPAs, or several Independent-JPAs and you facilitating an IC-JPA) focused on supporting and developing different aspects of the unit. The diagrams in Figure 6.3 illustrate four possible classroom structure arrangements you could use to begin grouping your students and incorporating IC-JPAs and Independent-JPAs. (After examining these classroom structures, complete the JPA: Benefits of Different Classroom Structure Configurations to begin to think about ways to incorporate these structures into your classroom.)

One last thought regarding the implementation of JPAs across the curricular disciplines. The strength of the pedagogical model presented in this

---

JPA TASK CARD: BENEFITS OF DIFFERENT CLASSROOM STRUCTURE CONFIGURATIONS

Instructional Goal

To promote thinking about how to choose a classroom structure that promotes and allows space for implementing Independent-JPAs and IC-JPAs in your classroom."

Task Activities

With your PLC:

- Examine the diagrams of classroom structure configurations in Figure 6.7.
- Create a T-Chart listing each of the configurations on the left side.
- Describe the benefits of each configuration on the right side of the chart.
- Give evidence for your decisions.

Questions to Consider

- How might intentional planning of your classroom structure impact your success in implementing JPAs?
- What factors should you consider when deciding on which structure you might use to get started?
- Once you choose your classroom structure, what factors might play in to your decision regarding how you might group your students within that structure?

---

book is that it can be applied to any curricular or disciplinary model—it is the *how*, not the *what*. In this lies the *power* of the Arch system.

Implications for School- and District-Level Administrators

Administrators recognize that it is challenging to create a new initiative in schools that will be implemented with fidelity and sustained over time, particularly when that initiative requires a paradigm shift in how we think about teaching, planning, and classroom interaction (as this system does). For those interested in rolling this pedagogical model out in their schools and districts, we have found, overall, that collaboration, sustained professional development, and administrative support are key to making this system thrive.

As echoed in the literature surrounding professional development approaches, the one-stop shop model that has teachers come in for a one-day workshop and then expect them to implement the new model with fidelity in their classroom is not the best way for sustained change in our schools (Darling-Hammond, Hyler, & Gardner, 2017). We have found that offering follow-up coaching and intermittent renewals (following an initial training on the theoretical and practical implications surrounding the model), as well as providing spaces to promote collaboration among teachers for planning and support purposes (see Gokee, 2017), are critical to promote fidelity of implementation and sustainability. Furthermore, teachers need to have their own safe environment to experiment with this model and ways it might work in their classroom, with support and understanding from their administration. As noted previously, this pedagogical system is not a "kit" or a "curriculum" to follow, but a change in the way we approach teaching in our classrooms. For this type of responsive teaching, collaboration and constant reflection are key; and providing spaces and times for that to happen for teachers, administrators, and district leaders is crucial to the success of this model.

References

Adloff, F., Gerund, K., & Kaldewey, D. (Eds.). (2015). *Revealing tacit knowledge: Embodiment and explication* (Presence & Tacit Knowledge, Vol. 2). Bielefeld, Germany: Transcript Verlag.

Azim, S., Gale, A., Lawlor-Wright, T., Kirkham, R., Khan, A., & Alam, M. (2010). The importance of soft skills in complex projects. *International Journal of Managing Projects in Business, 3*(3), 387–401.

Bellanca, J., & Brandt, R. (Eds.). (2010). *21st century skills: Rethinking how students learn.* Bloomington, IN: Solution Tree Press.

Bertolino, B., & O'Hanlon, W. H. (2002). *Collaborative, competency-based counseling and therapy.* Needham Heights, MA: Allyn and Bacon.

Bialystok, E., & Barac, R. (2012). Emerging bilingualism: Dissociating advantages for metalinguistic awareness and executive control. *Cognition, 122*(1), 67–73.

Billings, L., & Roberts, T. (2014). *Teaching critical thinking: Using seminars for 21st century literacy.* Routledge.

Bröchner, J. (2009). Construction metaphors in Aristotle: Knowledge, purpose, process. *Construction Management and Economics, 27*(5), 515–523.

Bruner, J. S. (1966). *Toward a theory of instruction* (Vol. 59). Cambridge, MA: Harvard University Press.

Bruner, J. S. (1975). The ontogenesis of speech acts. *Journal of Child Language, 2*(1), 1–19.

Bruner, J. S., & Haste, H. (Eds.). (2010). *Making sense (Routledge revivals): The child's construction of the world.* New York, NY: Routledge.

Callahan, R. M. (2005). Tracking and high school English learners: Limiting opportunity to learn. *American Educational Research Journal, 42*(2), 305–328.

Carroll, L. (2001). *Jabberwocky and other poems.* North Chelmsford, MA: Courier Corporation.

Celic, C., & Seltzer, K. (2011). Translanguaging: A CUNY-NYSIEB Guide for Educators. Retrieved from uiowa.edu/accel/sites/uiowa.edu.accel/files/wysiwyg_uploads/celicseltzer_translanguaging-guide-with-cover-1.pdf

Christenbury, L., & Kelly, P. P. (1983). *Questioning: A path to critical thinking.* Urbana, IL: National Council of Teachers of English. Retrieved from eric.ed.gov /?id=ED226372

Christie, F., & Maton, K. (Eds.). (2011). *Disciplinarity: Functional linguistic and sociological perspectives.* London, England: Bloomsbury.

Collins, A., Brown, J. S., & Newman, S. E. (1989). Cognitive apprenticeship: Teaching the crafts of reading, writing, and mathematics. In L. Resnick (Ed.),

Knowing, learning, and instruction: Essays in honor of Robert Glaser (pp. 453–491). Hillsdale, NY: Erlbaum.

Cormier, S., & Hackney, H. L. (2015). *Counseling strategies and interventions for professional helpers.* New York, NY: Pearson Higher Ed.

Cummins, J. (1980). The construct of language proficiency in bilingual education. In J. Alatis (Ed.), *Current issues in bilingual education* (pp. 81–103). Washington, DC: Georgetown University Press.

Cummins, J., Bismilla, V., Chow, P., Cohen, S., Giampapa, F., Leoni, L., Sandhu, P., & Sastri, P. (2005). Affirming identity in multilingual classrooms. *Educational Leadership, 63*(1), 38.

Dalton, S. S. (2008). *Five standards for effective teaching: How to succeed with all learners, grades K–8.* New York, NY: John Wiley & Sons.

Darling-Hammond, L., Hyler, M. E., & Gardner, M. (2017). *Effective teacher professional development.* Palo Alto, CA: Learning Policy Institute.

Darvin, R., & Norton, B. (2015). Identity and a model of investment in applied linguistics. *Annual Review of Applied Linguistics, 35*, 36–56.

Deming, D. J. (2017). The growing importance of social skills in the labor market. *The Quarterly Journal of Economics, 132*(4), 1593–1640.

Derry, S. J. (1996). Cognitive schema theory in the constructivist debate. *Educational Psychologist, 31*(3–4), 163–174.

Doll, B., Brehm, K., & Zucker, S. (2014). *Resilient classrooms: Creating healthy environments for learning.* New York, NY: Guilford Publications.

Donato, R. (1994). Collective scaffolding in second language learning. In Lantolf, J. & Appel, G. (Eds.) *Vygotskian approaches to second language research* (pp. 33–56). Norwood, NJ: Ablex.

Dörnyei, Z., & Ushioda, E. (2013). *Teaching and researching: Motivation.* London, UK, and New York, NY: Routledge.

Eelen, G. (2001). *A critique of politeness theory* (Vol. 1). London, UK: Routledge.

El Tatawy, M. (2002). Corrective feedback in second language acquisition. *Working Papers in TESOL & Applied Linguistics, 2*(2).

Ellis, R. (2008). A typology of written corrective feedback types. *ELT journal, 63*(2), 97-107.

Flanders, N. A. (1970). *Analyzing teaching behavior* (p. 34). Reading, MA: Addison-Wesley.

Flores, N. (2014, July 19). Let's not forget that translanguaging is a political act. [Blog post.] Retrieved from educationallinguist.wordpress.com/2014/07/19/lets-not-forget-that-translanguaging-is-a-political-act/

García, O., & Kleyn, T. (2016). *Translanguaging with multilingual students: Learning from classroom moments.* New York, NY: Routledge.

Gardner, R. C., Masgoret, A. M., Tennant, J., & Mihic, L. (2004). Integrative motivation: Changes during a year-long intermediate-level language course. *Language Learning, 54*(1), 1–34.

Gass, S. M. (2013). *Second language acquisition: An introductory course.* London, UK: Routledge.

Gibbons, P. (2009). *English learners, academic literacy, and thinking: Learning in the challenge zone.* Portsmouth, NH: Heinemann.

Goffman, E. (1974). *Frame analysis: An essay on the organization of experience.* Cambridge, MA: Harvard University Press.

Gokee, R. K. (2017). Improving reading achievement of ELLs one conversation at a time: Implementation of the IC model in upper elementary school classrooms—Voices from the field (Unpublished doctoral dissertation). University of Georgia, Athens, GA.

González, N., Moll, L. C., & Amanti, C. (Eds.). (2006). *Funds of knowledge: Theorizing practices in households, communities, and classrooms.* New York, NY: Routledge.

Graham, S. (2006). Listening comprehension: The learners' perspective. *System, 34*(2), 165–182.

Grube, D., Ryan, S., Lowell, S., & Stringer, A. (2018). Effective classroom management in physical education: Strategies for beginning teachers. *Journal of Physical Education, Recreation & Dance, 89*(8), 47–52.

Hardmeier, C. (2015, Sept.). *On statistical machine translation and translation theory.* Paper presented at the Association for Computational Linguistics Second Workshop on Discourse in Machine Translation (DiscoMT), 17 September 2015, Lisbon, Portugal. Retrieved from www.emnlp2015.org/proceedings/DiscoMT/pdf/DiscoMT22.pdf

Hartshorn, K. J., Evans, N. W., Merrill, P. F., Sudweeks, R. R., Strong-Krause, D., & Anderson, N. J. (2010). Effects of dynamic corrective feedback on ESL writing accuracy. *Tesol Quarterly, 44*(1), 84–109.

Hattie, J. (2008). *Visible learning: A synthesis of over 800 meta-analyses relating to achievement.* New York, NY: Routledge.

Hattie, J. A., & Donoghue, G. M. (2016). Learning strategies: A synthesis and conceptual model. *npj Science of Learning, 1*, id. 16013. doi: http://dx.doi.org/10.1038/npjscilearn.2016.13

Headlee, C. (2017). *We need to talk: How to have conversations that matter.* London, UK: Hachette UK.

Hoey, M. (2012). *Lexical priming: A new theory of words and language.* London; New York, NY: Routledge.

Hooker, S., Fix, M., & McHugh, M. (2014). *Education reform in a changing Georgia: Promoting high school and college success for immigrant youth.* Migration Policy Institute. Washington, DC.

Hoppe, M. (2006). *Active listening: Improve your ability to listen and lead.* Center for Creative Leadership.

Hudson, J. M., & Bruckman, A. S. (2002). IRC Francais: The creation of an Internet-based SLA community. *Computer Assisted Language Learning, 15*(2), 109–134.

Hurrell, S. A. (2016). Rethinking the soft skills deficit blame game: Employers, skills withdrawal and the reporting of soft skills gaps. *Human Relations, 69*(3), 605–628.

Ibrahim, A. E. K. M. (1999). Becoming black: Rap and hip-hop, race, gender, identity, and the politics of ESL learning. *TESOL Quarterly, 33*(3), 349–369.

Immordino-Yang, M. H., & Damasio, A. (2007). We feel, therefore we learn: The relevance of affective and social neuroscience to education. *Mind, Brain, and Education, 1*(1), 3–10.

Jackson, R. R., & Lambert, C. (2010). *How to support struggling students (Mastering the Principles of Great Teaching* series). Alexandria, VA: ASCD.

Jacobs, E. E., Masson, R. L., Harvill, R. L., & Schimmel, C. J. (2011). *Group counseling: Strategies and skills.* Boston, MA: Cengage.

Johnson, D., & Johnson, R. (2009). Energizing learning: The instructional power of conflict. *Educational Researcher, 38,* 37–51.

Kalman, M. (2014). *Thomas Jefferson: Life, liberty and the pursuit of everything.* New York, NY: Penguin.

Kirova, A., & Jamison, N. M. (2018). Peer scaffolding techniques and approaches in preschool children's multiliteracy practices with iPads. *Journal of Early Childhood Research, 16*(3), 245–257. doi: 10.1177/1476718X18775762

Kormos, J. (2014). *Speech production and second language acquisition.* New York, NY: Routledge.

Kozulin A., Gindis B., Ageyev V. S., & Miller S. M. (Eds.) (2003) Vygotsky's Educational Theory in Cultural Context, Cambridge University Press, Cambridge.

Krashen, S. D. (1985). *The input hypothesis: Issues and implications.* New York, NY: Addison-Wesley Longman Ltd.

Kruglanski, A. W., & Gigerenzer, G. (2018). Intuitive and deliberate judgments are based on common principles. In A. Kruglanski, *The motivated mind: The selected works of Arie Kruglanski* (pp. 112–136). New York, NY: Routledge.

Kuhn, D. (2015). Thinking together and alone. *Educational Researcher, 44*(1), 46–53.

Lantolf, J. P. (2011). The sociocultural approach to second language acquisition: Sociocultural theory, second language acquisition, and artificial L2 development. In *Alternative approaches to second language acquisition* (pp. 36–59). New York, NY: Routledge.

Lantolf, J. P., Thorne, S. L., & Poehner, M. E. (2015). Sociocultural theory and second language development. In B. Van Patten & J. Williams (Eds.), *Theories in second language acquisition: An introduction* (pp. 207–226). New York, NY: Routledge.

Lave, J., & Wenger, E. (1991). *Situated learning: Legitimate peripheral participation.* Cambridge, England: Cambridge University Press.

Leech, G. N. (1983). *Principles of pragmatics.* London/New York: Longman.

Liew, J. (2012). Effortful control, executive functions, and education: Bringing self-regulatory and social-emotional competencies to the table. *Child Development Perspectives, 6*(2), 105–111.

Lightbown, P. M., & Spada, N., (2013). *How languages are learned* (fourth ed.). Oxford: Oxford University Press.

Long, M. (1983). Does second language instruction make a difference? A review of research. *TESOL Quarterly, 17*(3), 359–382.

Long, M. (2014). *Second language acquisition and task-based language teaching.* John Wiley & Sons.

Lowry, L. (1989). *Number the stars.* New York, NY: Houghton Mifflin Harcourt.

Lyster, R. (2017). *Content-based language teaching.* New York, NY: Routledge.

Mandler, J. M. (2014). *Stories, scripts, and scenes: Aspects of schema theory.* New York, NY: Psychology Press.

McFarlin, K. (2013). The importance of soft skills in the workplace. *Chron. com.* Retrieved from: smallbusiness.chron.com/importance-soft-skills-workplace-10111.html

McKay, S. L., & Wong, S. L. C. (1996). Multiple discourses, multiple identities: Investment and agency in second-language learning among Chinese adolescent immigrant students. *Harvard Educational Review, 66*(3), 577–609.

Moll, L. C., Amanti, C., Neff, D., & González, N. (1992). Funds of knowledge for teaching: Using a qualitative approach to connect homes and classrooms. *Theory into Practice, 31*(2), 132–141.

National Clearinghouse for English Language Acquisition (NCELA). Office of English Language Acquisition, Language Enhancement, and Academic Achievement for Limited English Proficient Students. (2017). *Georgia demographics and state data.* Retrieved from ncela.ed.gov/t3sis/Georgia.php

National Clearinghouse for English Language Acquisition (NCELA). (2018). National Clearinghouse for English Language Acquisition. Retrieved from ncela. ed.gov/files/fast_facts/LEAs_Fact_Sheet_2018_Final.pdf

National Center for Education Statistics. (2015). *The condition of education.* Washington DC: US Department of Education.

Newkirk, T., & McLure, P. (1992). *Listening in: Children talk about books (and other things).* Portsmouth, NH: Heinemann.

Oakley, B., Felder, R. M., Brent, R., & Elhajj, I. (2004). Turning student groups into effective teams. *Journal of Student Centered Learning, 2*(1), 9–34.

Olsen, J. K., & Finkelstein, S. (2017). *Through the (thin-slice) looking glass: An initial look at rapport and co-construction within peer collaboration.* Philadelphia, PA: International Society of the Learning Sciences.

Passel, J. S., Cohn, D. V., & Lopez, M. H. (2011). *Hispanics account for more than half of nation's growth in past decade* (pp. 1–7). Washington, DC: Pew Hispanic Center.

Patrick, B. C., Hisley, J., & Kempler, T. (2000). "What's everybody so excited about?": The effects of teacher enthusiasm on student intrinsic motivation and vitality. *The Journal of Experimental Education, 68*(3), 217–236.

Payton, J., Weissberg, R. P., Durlak, J. A., Dymnicki, A. B., Taylor, R. D., Schellinger, K. B., & Pachan, M. (2008). *The positive impact of social and emotional learning for kindergarten to eighth-grade students: Findings from three scientific reviews.* Chicago, IL: Collaborative for Academic, Social, and Emotional Learning.

Perin, D. (2011). Facilitating student learning through contextualization: A review of evidence. *Community College Review, 39*(3), 268–295.

Pianta, R. C., Belsky, J., Vandergrift, N., Houts, R., & Morrison, F. J. (2008). Classroom effects on children's achievement trajectories in elementary school. *American Educational Research Journal, 45*(2), 365–397.

Portes, P. R., González Canché, M., Boada, D., & Whatley, M. E. (2018). Early evaluation findings from the instructional conversation study: Culturally responsive teaching outcomes for diverse learners in elementary school. *American Educational Research Journal, 55*(3), 488–531.

Ranjbar, N., & Ghonsooly, B. (2017). Peer scaffolding behaviors emerging in revising a written task: A microgenetic analysis. *Iranian Journal of Language Teaching Research, 5*(2), 75–90.

Rickel, J., & Johnson, W. L. (2000). Task-oriented collaboration with embodied agents in virtual worlds. In J. Cassell, J. Sullivan, & S. Prevost (Eds.), *Embodied conversational agents* (pp. 95–122). Boston, MA: MIT Press.

Robles, M. M. (2012). Executive perceptions of the top 10 soft skills needed in today's workplace. *Business Communication Quarterly, 75*(4), 453–465.

Rymes, B. (2014). *Communicating beyond language: Everyday encounters with diversity.* New York, NY: Routledge.

Schank, R. C., & Ableson, R. P. (1995). Knowledge and memory: The real story. In. R. S. Wyer (Ed.), *Knowledge and memory: The real story* (pp. 1–85). New York: Psychology Press.

Schudson, M. (1997). Why conversation is not the soul of democracy. *Critical Studies in Media Communication, 14*(4), 297–309.

Scollon, R., & Scollon, S. B. (1981). *Narrative, literacy and face in interethnic communication (Vol. 7).* Norwood, NJ: Ablex Publishing Corporation.

Sheen, Y. (2010). Differential effects of oral and written corrective feedback in the ESL classroom. *Studies in Second Language Acquisition, 32*(2), 203–234.

Shenk, D. (2011). *The genius in all of us: New Insights into genetics, talent, and IQ.* New York, NY: Anchor.

Sinclair, J. M. (Ed.). (1987). *Looking up: An account of the COBUILD project in lexical computing and the development of the Collins COBUILD English language dictionary.* New York, NY: Harper Collins.

Sollinger, E. & Rallis, C. (2014). *Owls: Birds of the night.* New York, NY: Penguin.

Stewart, J. (1983). Interpretive listening: An alternative to empathy. *Communication Education, 32*(4), 379–391.

Swain, M., Brooks, L., & Tocalli-Beller, A. (2002). Peer-peer dialogue as a means of second language. *Annual Review of Applied Linguistics, 22,* 171–185.

Swain, M., & Lapkin, S. (1995). Problems in output and the cognitive processes they generate: A step towards second language learning. *Applied Linguistics, 16*(3), 371–391.

Swain, M., & Watanabe, Y. (2012). Languaging: Collaborative dialogue as a source of second language learning. *The encyclopedia of applied linguistics.* Retrieved from dcdc.coe.hawaii.edu/ltec/612/wp-content/uploads/2014/07/Communicative-Language-Teaching.pdf

Tannen, D., Hamilton, H. E., & Schiffrin, D. (2015). *The handbook of discourse analysis.* New York, NY: John Wiley & Sons.

Teasley, S. D. (1997). Talking about reasoning: How important is the peer in peer collaboration? In L. B. Resnick, R. Säljö, C. Pontecorvo, & B. Burge (Eds.), *Discourse, tools and reasoning* (pp. 361–384). Berlin & Heidelberg, Germany: Springer.

Tharp, R. G., Estrada, P., Dalton, S. S., & Yamauchi, L. (2000). *Teaching transformed: Achieving excellence, fairness, inclusion, and harmony.* Boulder, CO: Westview Press.

Thomson, D. S. (2006). The Sapir-Whorf hypothesis: Worlds shaped by words. In J. P. Spradley & D. W. McCurdy (Eds.), *Conformity and conflict: Readings in cultural anthropology* (12th ed., pp. 113–125). New York, NY: Allyn & Bacon.

Thorne, S. L., & Lantolf, J. P. (2007). A linguistics of communicative activity. *Disinventing and reconstituting languages, 62,* 170–195.

Turkle, S. (2017). *Alone together: Why we expect more from technology and less from each other* (rev. ed.). New York, NY: Basic Books.

U.S. Census Bureau (2010). The Hispanic population: 2010. Washington, DC: U.S. Department of Commerce.

Van Lier, L. (2014). *Interaction in the language curriculum: Awareness, autonomy and authenticity.* New York, NY: Routledge.

Vygotsky, L.S. (1978). *Mind in society: The development of higher psychological processes,* Cole, M., John-Steiner, V., Scribner, S., & Soberman, E. (Eds.). Cambridge, MA: Harvard University Press.

Waddell, M. (2012). *Owl babies.* Somerville, MA: Candlewick Press.

Walqui, A. (2006). Scaffolding instruction for English language learners: A conceptual framework. *International Journal of Bilingual Education and Bilingualism,* 9(2), 159–180.

Watanabe, Y., & Swain, M. (2007). Effects of proficiency differences and patterns of pair interaction on second language learning: Collaborative dialogue between adult ESL learners. *Language teaching research,* 11(2), 121–142.

Webb, N. M., Franke, M. L., Ing, M., Turrou, A. C., Johnson, N. C., & Zimmerman, J. (2017). Teacher practices that promote productive dialogue and learning in mathematics classrooms. *International Journal of Educational Research.* doi.org/10.1016/j.ijer.2017.07.009

Wenger, E., & Lave, J. (2001). Legitimate peripheral participation in communities of practice. In J. Clarke, A. Hanson, R. Harrison, & F. Reeve (Eds.) *Supporting lifelong learning, Vol. I: Perspectives in Learning* (pp. 121–136). London, UK: Routledge.

Wong, H. K., Wong, R. T., & Seroyer, C. (2005). *The first days of school: How to be an effective teacher.* Mountain View, CA: Harry K. Wong Publications.

Wray, A. (2005). *Formulaic language and the lexicon.* Cambridge, UK: Cambridge University Press.

Wray, A., & Bloomer, A. (2013). *Projects in linguistics and language studies.* New York: Routledge.

Xia, T., Xu, G., & Mo, L. (2018). Bi-lateralized Whorfian effect in color perception: Evidence from Chinese Sign Language. *Journal of Neurolinguistics, 49,* 189–201. doi: 10.1016/j.jneuroling.2018.07.004

Yolen, J. (1987). *Owl moon.* New York, NY: Penguin.

Zwiers, J., & Crawford, M. (2011). *Academic conversations: Classroom talk that fosters critical thinking and content understandings.* Portsmouth, NH: Stenhouse.

Index

About the Authors

Paula J. Mellom is the associate director of the Center for Latino Achievement and Success in Education (CLASE) at the University of Georgia's (UGA) College of Education and affiliate faculty in UGA's Departments of Linguistics and Language and Literacy. She has a PhD in linguistics and more than 30 years' experience as a teacher educator and as a teacher of linguistically and culturally diverse learners in both the United States and Central America.

Rebecca K. Hixon is a postdoctoral research and teaching associate at University of Georgia in the College of Education's Center for Latino Achievement and Success in Education (CLASE). She has a PhD in educational psychology with a focus in applied cognition and development. As a former classroom teacher and current teacher educator, she has more than a decade of experience working with students and teachers in both the United States and abroad.

Jodi P. Weber is the assistant director of professional development for the Center for Latino Achievement and Success in Education (CLASE) and faculty in the University of Georgia's (UGA) College of Education. She has an EdS in emotional behavioral disorders and educational leadership and over 39 years of experience as a special education teacher, school administrator, and teacher educator.